Controversies in Sociology
edited by
Professor T. B. Bottomore and Professor M. J. Mulkay

13
Positivism and Sociology:
Explaining Social Life

Controversies in Sociology

Positivism and Sociology: Explaining Social Life

PETER HALFPENNY
University of Manchester

London
GEORGE ALLEN & UNWIN
Boston   Sydney

George Allen & Unwin (Publishers) Ltd,
40 Museum Street, London WC1A 1LU, UK

George Allen & Unwin (Publishers) Ltd,
Park Lane, Hemel Hempstead, Herts HP2 4TE, UK

Allen & Unwin, Inc.,
9 Winchester Terrace, Winchester, Mass. 01890, USA

George Allen & Unwin Australia Pty Ltd,
8 Napier Street, North Sydney, NSW 2060, Australia

First published in 1982

Library of Congress Cataloging in Publication Data
Halfpenny, Peter.
  Positivism and sociology.
(Controversies in sociology ; 13)
Bibliography: p.
Includes index.
1. Sociology—History. 2. Positivism. 3. Sociology—Methodology.
I. Title.   II. Series.
HM19.H18 1982   301   82–11558
ISBN 0-04-300084-3
ISBN 0-04-300085-1 (pbk.)

Set in 11 on 12 point Times by Typesetters (Birmingham) Ltd
and printed in Great Britain
by Billing & Sons Ltd, London and Worcester

Contents

Acknowledgements

I have learned much from Isabel Emmett, Len Gill, Keekok Imber, Richard Whitley, Philippe Van Parijs and especially Daphne Taylorson, who all read and offered me comments on the draft, and I thank them for their time and interest. I am grateful too to Tom Bottomore and Mike Mulkay for their encouragement and advice, and to Jeanne Ashton, Tricia Pygott, Janice Hammond and Hilary Thornber for their excellent typing.

Introduction

Controversy over positivism begins immediately 'positivism' is used, for there are so many different understandings about how the term can or should be used. There are differences that depend upon whether the term is used to label oneself or one's enemies, for the positivism of positivists differs from the positivism of anti-positivists. There are differences among anti-positivists, who use the term loosely and indiscriminately to describe all sorts of disfavoured forms of inquiry. And there are differences even among positivists themselves, for they have continually developed and changed the central ideas out of which they have fashioned various forms of positivism at different historical times.

In sociology, allegiances to or accusations of positivism are made in a wealth of different ways. Sometimes, to be positivist means no more than to be scientific in some undisclosed manner, although that fails to discriminate between positivism and all the other sociologies that have claims to be scientific in perhaps different ways, such as Marxism, functionalism, structuralism, and so on. Sometimes, positivist sociology is synonymous with statistical analysis, as in many sociological research reports and methods textbooks. Sometimes, to practise positivist sociology is to seek to establish causal explanations, or to search for fundamental laws of human behaviour or historical change, or to insist upon objective empirical information systematically organised to generate or test hypotheses.

The existence of these diverse understandings of 'positivism', among others, reveals that the issue of what positivism is, and was, remains controversial. It is with this controversy that most of the following pages are concerned. My principal aim is to identify some of the most important uses of the term 'positivism', and to describe some of the different positivisms that have emerged at different times since the mid-nineteenth century. Only when different understandings of 'positivism' have been systematically elucidated and evaluated can other related controversies be joined, such as whether and in what sense positivism is dead or alive, and whether the enormous influence of various forms of positivism over sociology has been beneficial or malign.

My discussion takes the following form. In Chapter 1 I explore the first of the two roots of twentieth-century sociological positivism – French positive philosophy as captured in the works of Comte. In Chapter 2 I examine the second, quite distinct root in statistics. In the third chapter I turn to the philosophy of the logical positivists, which in many ways defined the subsequent programme for twentieth-century philosophy of the natural and social sciences. Developments in the details of this programme are discussed in the two chapters that follow. Chapter 4 charts the changing positivist conceptions of laws and explanation, centring on problems involved in defining science in terms of the quest for causes. Chapter 5 considers changes in positivist conceptions both of what constitutes evidence – the empirical base of science – and of how theory is built upon or otherwise related to this base. In the Conclusion I reflect upon the different understandings of the term positivism identified in the previous chapters, and conclude with some remarks about current debates among philosophers of the natural and social sciences, and about contemporary responses to controversies over positivism in sociology.

1

Comte and the Early Period

The name 'positivist philosophy' was originally coined by the Parisian Auguste Comte (1798–1857) to describe his systematic reconstruction of the history and development of scientific knowledge. His ideas were initially sketched out in essays (1822, 1824), and then presented comprehensively in a series of lectures, the 'Cours de philosophie positive', begun in 1826 and completed in 1829, and then published in six volumes over the years 1830 to 1842. Positivist knowledge, Comte maintained, was the inevitable outcome both of the progressive growth of the individual mind and of the historical development of human knowledge. Comte believed that in his extensive reading over the whole range of scientific disciplines he had discovered a great and fundamental historical law, his famous law of three stages. According to this law, individual thinkers in all branches of knowledge necessarily begin by accounting for phenomena theologically, by explaining mundane occurrences as willed by unfathomable gods. This is the necessary starting point of all knowledge for two reasons. First, without some theoretical guide one could not begin to make systematic observations (for there would be no way of discriminating between important or theory-relevant observations and unimportant ones), and it is, according to Comte, theological theories which arise spontaneously in the primitive human mind. Secondly, sciences in their infancy research the most intractable questions, about the essences of phenomena and their ultimate origins and destinies, to which theological answers are most appropriate.

Theology provides the attractive chimera that excites curiosity and stimulates intellectual inquiry, but this first stage of knowledge is inevitably followed by the second, metaphysical stage, where it is not spiritual agents but abstract forces, powers and essences that are posited as responsible for worldly affairs. This second stage is a necessary transitional interlude, a period of negative criticism of the first theological epoch, before the appearance of the third and final positive or scientific era. Here, unresolvable issues about ultimate origins, inaccessible powers and final purposes are relinquished in favour of the more limited but attainable end of describing relations observed to hold between phenomena. 'The fundamental character of the positive philosophy is to consider all phenomena as subject to invariable natural laws. The exact discovery of these laws and their reduction to the least possible number constitutes the goal of all our efforts' (Comte, 1830, p. 8). The Newtonian law of gravitation is, for Comte, the paradigm case of a positive law. It provides the standard against which to measure the maturity of all fields of inquiry, and the ideal they should seek to emulate.

In their rate of development, Comte argues, the sciences fall into a natural order, his hierarchy of the sciences. The lower sciences develop first: a form of inquiry progresses to the positive stage at a rate that is greater the less complex it is, the less its dependence on other sciences, and the greater its distance from human affairs. In his *Cours* Comte presented a vast review of contemporary knowledge to show that astronomy (celestial physics), mechanics and chemistry (terrestrial physics) and biology or physiology (organic physics) had arrived at the positive stage, in that order, and he concluded that all that remained to complete the system of the observational sciences was to found the positive science of society, which he originally called social physics, but for which he later coined the name sociology. This task he set himself to accomplish.

Notable for its absence from his hierarchy of sciences is psychology, which Comte rejected as a metaphysical remnant because, he argued, 'interior observation' of intellectual phenomena, on which the psychology of his day was based, is not possible, for 'the thinking individual cannot cut himself in two – one of the parts reasoning, while the other is looking on' (Comte, 1830, p. 21). Even if it were possible, it is not an objective source of knowledge of mental phenomena, for 'it gives rise to almost as many divergent opinions as there are so-called observers' (ibid., p. 22). Encouraged by the phrenology of Franz Joseph Gall (1758–1828), Comte believed that psychology would be replaced by 'cerebral physiology', which gave mental operations a physical location in the brain and put an end to metaphysical speculations about thought being the essence of the soul.

For Comte, sociology was the queen of the sciences, for without the guidance of its laws, the discoveries of the lower sciences could not be utilised to their maximum advantage for humanity. But although Comte's avowed aim in the *Cours* was to construct positive sociology, the natural science of society, his study is in the main devoted to arguing that the fulfilment of this aim is possible and necessary. He does not there present any newly discovered empirical sociological laws, other than the law of three stages (and the empirical justification for that law was doubted by later writers).

As propounded in the *Cours*, Comte's positive philosophy has three parts, and it provides the first three conceptions of positivism. Positivism$_1$ is a theory of historical development in which improvements in knowledge are both the motor of historical progress and the source of social stability. Positivism$_2$ is a theory of knowledge, according to which the only kind of sound knowledge available to humankind is that of science, grounded in observation. Positivism$_3$ is a unity of science thesis, according to which all sciences can be integrated into a single natural system.

Comte's achievement lay in bringing together under the

new name of 'positivism' a variety of themes current in early nineteenth-century thought, themes which stemmed from the eighteenth-century French Enlightenment and the conservative reaction to it. Indeed, in Comte's eyes, it is the Enlightenment that constitutes the metaphysical stage, the period of negative criticism of the old theological order, that paves the way for the new positive scientific age.

The most obvious Enlightenment theme in Comte's *Cours* is the belief in the power of human reason to grasp the workings of the world and, concomitantly, the rejection of the traditional teachings of the church that reality is knowable only by and through God. Moreover, the world that is within the reach of human reason includes both nature and humanity. No longer was it accepted that human beings, because they are potentially spiritual (or for any other reason), are discontinuous with brute nature. All phenomena, natural, mental and social, are equally amenable to human investigation. But although Comte concurred with the Enlightenment *philosophes* that it is necessary to break with the idea that knowledge is constituted by divine decree (Becker, 1932; Nisbet, 1973), his positive philosophy marked the end of philosophy in the traditional sense of metaphysics, of analysis that goes beyond physics, beyond the science of observable reality. He could not agree with the radical Cartesian rationalists of the Enlightenment when they claimed that knowledge was the result of deductions from 'self-evident dictates of pure reason', that human thought alone, freed from theological interference, could construct knowledge. Rather, Comte insisted, thought must be guided by experience, reason subjugated to reality. Any suggestion that there are *a priori* principles that guarantee knowledge is mere speculation. It is empirical evidence that secures knowledge. Positive philosophy restricts itself to the empirical study of this empirical knowledge, with the aim of formulating laws like any other positive science. Comte's own study in the *Cours* of the history of the sciences, culminating in his law of three stages, is a prime example of this new positive philosophical attitude.

The knowledge that human experience reveals is unified, and the division of phenomena into different disciplines is an arbitrary convenience. Although the sciences arrive at the ultimate positive stage at different times, there are no essential differences between branches of knowledge. This theme, too, Comte took from the eighteenth-century *philosophes*, who, collaborating under the editorship of Denis Diderot (1713–84) and Jean le Rond D'Alembert (1717–83), sought to compile a systematic compendium unifying all prevailing ideas in the arts, sciences and crafts. Comte's *Cours* is a descendant of their twenty-eight volume *Encyclopédie*, published over the period 1751–72 (Hazard, 1954).

Despite founding and unifying knowledge in human experience, Comte disapproved of the Enlightenment thinkers' celebration of the individual, which he believed was the source of the post-revolutionary crisis of civilisation in France and other European countries. Individualism, which he described as the disease of Western civilisation, fails to recognise that social order, and society itself, rest on moral consensus, on an organic unity, and any attempt to understand society by dissecting it into its component individuals is fatal. Although opposed to religion as a theory of knowledge, Comte recognised the importance of religion as a unifying moral force. Given the contemporary challenges to religious authority, the answer to social upheavals, thought Comte, lay in the moral regeneration of the population by strengthening existing institutions such as the family and providing new ones such as a scientific (positivist) leadership. Interestingly, despite his belief that re-establishing social stability requires that individuals submit to the moral regulation of the group, Comte did not provide a theory of the state or of other specifically political institutions. He shared in the growing nineteenth-century realisation that society was more than the state (Runciman, 1965), and so his positive philosophy was not a science of politics, analysing the origin and uses of government, but a science of society in general.

In his antagonism to individualism, Comte sided with

the conservatives such as Joseph de Maistre (1753–1821) and Louis de Bonald (1754–1840) in their reaction against the *philosophes* (Nisbet, 1967). Yet Comte was no conservative, harking back to the old order. Following Anne Robert Jacques Turgot (1727–81) and the Marquis de Condorcet (1743–94), he believed in the necessity and desirability of progress, which was to be achieved in exactly the same way that order was established: through the development and application of scientific knowledge (Becker and Barnes, 1938, ch. 13). Just as nature had been tamed once its laws were known, so societal disorder was to be controlled by discovering the laws which govern its course. Social conflict is due to ignorance, and it is overcome when people learn the laws of society and learn to accommodate to them. Only on the basis of empirical sociological laws, Comte insisted, could social harmony be established and social reforms rationally planned and introduced, and the disorder that results from attempting to fulfil impossible aspirations, among which he included individual liberty, be avoided. Comte's positive sociology was a science of stability *and* social reconstruction. It linked together order and progress, which earlier had been thought to be implacably opposed.

In sum, for Comte the enemies of positive philosophy were religion (as a dogma, not as a moral system), metaphysics (in which he included psychology), individualism and revolutionary utopianism. Religion made the world mysterious and so inhibited empirical inquiry. Metaphysical speculations were uncontrolled by experience and so disputes between rival opinions were undecidable and of no practical value to humankind. Psychology was founded on unreliable self-knowledge gained through introspection. Individualism made the mistake of suggesting that society could be constructed by individuals, and failed to recognise that individuals are constituted by society. Revolutionary utopians dreamed up visions of society that took no account of what science revealed to be possible or impossible.

In opposition to these ideas, Comte's positive philosophy was empiricist, sociologistic, encyclopaedic, scientistic and progressivist: empiricist because human experience was the arbiter of knowledge; sociologistic because psychological study of human subjectivity was ousted by sociological study of social phenomena, which precede and constitute the individual psyche (Benoit-Smullyan, 1948); encyclopaedic (or naturalistic) because all the sciences, natural and human, can be integrated into a unified system of natural laws; scientistic because knowledge has practical value and the growth of science is for the benefit of humankind; progressivist (or social reformist) because the crisis of civilisation could be solved and social stability restored by adjusting human desires to the scientifically established laws of society, by re-establishing a scientifically based supra-individual moral order to replace the deposed authority of the Catholic Church.

It is these features of Comte's system, or a selection from them, that are today identified as having had the most significant influence on his contemporaries and successors, rather than any substantive contributions he might have made to what is nowadays meant by sociology. This is for a number of reasons. One is that, despite his antipathy towards utopianism and cosmogony, Comte's science of society consisted of a millenarian cosmology, a universal history of humankind, culminating in predictions about the perfectibility of society if people were prepared to submit themselves to science. Since Comte's death in the middle of the nineteenth century sociology has become more specialised, more narrowly construed as the study of the structured social relations that constitute social institutions and societies: it has been separated from general social philosophy. The contrast between the present conception of sociology and Comte's more grandiose science of social reform is most pronounced when considering his later work, especially the four-volume *Système de politique positive* (1851–4), where positivism took on another form, separate from both the theory of history and the theory of knowledge that it had earlier been. The *Système* embodies positivism$_4$ which is a secular religion of humanity devoted to the worship of society, to be promulgated and administered by the priesthood of the positivist church, headed by Comte as high priest. Although this movement was popular with some of his followers (W. M. Simon, 1963), for others it was an aberration that violated the precepts of positive science that Comte himself had expounded in his earlier work.

This latter was the view, in particular, of John Stuart Mill (1806–73), the English empiricist philosopher, who had been impressed by Comte's *Cours* and had been responsible for introducing its ideas to British audiences. Although he dissented from Comte's sociologism, being a staunch defender of empirical psychology and individual liberty, Mill agreed with Comte that the study of society had been retarded by its failure to employ scientific methods. Mill also agreed that the goal of science was the production of laws summarising the regular association of phenomena. Consequently, he was in sympathy with the empirical methods of data collection that Comte recommended: observation, experiment, comparison and, unique to sociology, historical method, through which the units compared in the comparative method are assembled into an historical progression. But Mill felt that Comte had paid insufficient attention to methods of data analysis, specifically the logic of induction through which the truth of laws is empirically justified. The *Cours* prompted Mill to complete his *System of Logic* (1843), a study of the methods used to justify laws, particularly in the moral sciences (see Chapter 5). Mill's early enthusiasm for Comte's work faded, however, as Comte came to concentrate increasingly on the religion of humanity, and by the time the eighth edition of the *System of Logic* was published in 1872 Mill had removed most of his favourable references to Comte (W. M. Simon, 1963).

Another reason why Comte's abstract philosophical ideas are generally considered more important than his substantive sociological ideas is that his speculative pronouncements about progress and the moral reconstruction of society were soon overtaken in popularity by the evolutionary sociology of Herbert Spencer (1820–1903), which was widely understood to offer a scientific corrective to Comte's later pseudo-religious excesses. Spencer's evolutionism, when first expounded in the 1850s, dovetailed with the *laissez-faire* ethos of the day. His ideas formed part of the general movement now known as social Darwinism (Hofstadter, 1955), after the famous account of evolution by Charles Darwin (1809–92) in *On the Origin of Species* published in 1859 – though Spencer's first statement of evolution antedated Darwin's book by several years (Peel, 1971). Spencer disagreed with many of Comte's ideas, and claimed to be little influenced by him (Spencer, 1864). In particular, being committed to individual responsibility, he abhorred the moral authoritarianism of Comte's sociology. The earlier progressivists, including Comte, had claimed that progress relied upon increasing social harmony – avoiding conflict and competition – by subjugating individuals to the moral order, by imposing science over individuality. Spencer rejected this sociologism, and instead proposed an individualistic theory of historical development in which competition between individuals was the motor of progress. (Marx and Engels were developing a theory of progress that depended on conflict between classes rather than individuals at about the same time.) The very competition which Comte took to be the result of either ignorance of the harmonising laws of society or failure to conform to them was for Spencer the manifestation of real incompatibilities between individuals' interests (or for Marx, classes' interests), and the struggle of one against another provided the internal dynamic for the advance of society.

Despite his differences from Comte, Spencer is commonly considered to have reinforced the 'positivist spirit' of the second half of the nineteenth century and is often identified as one of the important sources of twentieth-century sociological positivism (Timasheff, 1955; Martindale, 1961; Kolakowski, 1966). Consequently, his work is taken to provide a fifth conception of positivism: positivism$_5$ is a theory of history in which the motor of progress that guarantees the emergence of superior forms of society is competition between increasingly differentiated individuals.

Spencer's evolutionary theory of history (positivism$_5$) is opposed to Comte's theory of history (positivism$_1$), but what links the two authors is their naturalism (positivism$_3$), for just as Comte unifies all knowledge in his hierarchy of sciences, so Spencer unifies all knowledge under his principle of evolution. Although evolutionary theories can form the basis of anti-naturalism (and therefore anti-positivism$_3$) if interpreted teleologically in terms of the wilful pursuit of human goals, Spencer's universal evolutionary principle is a naturalistic one: he maintains that because every active force or cause produces more than one effect, progress in all areas – physical, biological and human – consists in increasing differentiation, passing from homogeneity to heterogeneity. Accordingly, social development is a purely natural process, and not the product of individual will or human goal-seeking (Spencer, 1857).

Spencer was also sympathetic to the scientistic notion, supported by Comte, that society would benefit if the organisation of social life were guided by science, and not by either traditional (religious) beliefs or irrational utopian ideals. Unlike Comte, however, Spencer included among the utopian ideals to be eschewed in favour of science those reformist sentiments that encouraged intervention in the course of history to mitigate the misfortunes of others. This theme was enthusiastically endorsed by the British eugenicists, such as Francis Galton (1822–1911) and Karl Pearson (1857–1936), who have an important place in the history of sociology, partly because their extreme views fragmented and factionalised British sociology and so delayed and deformed its academic institutionalisation as an independent discipline (P. Abrams, 1968), and partly because they developed the modern techniques of statistical analysis that were to play a central role in later conceptions of positivist sociology (MacKenzie, 1979).

Spencer, especially in his later writings, was less uncompromising in his competitive individualism than the eugenicists who followed him. He believed that a necessary outcome of evolutionary progress would be a growth in altruism at the expense of the egoism which underlay *laissez-faire* doctrines (Hawthorne, 1976). When this failed to occur and when, towards the end of the nineteenth century, it became apparent to many that liberal capitalism did not, unaided (that is naturally), engender moral goodness, social Darwinism came under increasing attack. Social reformers, dismayed by its destructive political and social consequences revealed by their social surveys, believed progress would be achieved not by protecting the natural process of individualistic competition from irrational interference, but only by active intervention to ameliorate its damaging effects.

Interest in Spencerian sociology had evaporated by the 1930s, even in America where it had been most favourably received (Parsons, 1937). Comtean ideas and ideals found a more lasting embodiment in the form of sociology that Emile Durkheim (1858–1917) was instrumental in establishing as an academic discipline in French universities at the beginning of the twentieth century (Clark, 1973). Durkheim was quite explicit in acknowledging his debt to Comte (Tiryakian, 1979), and it is largely mediated by Durkheim that Comte has whatever importance he does for modern sociology. In general, Durkheim adopted all of Comte's major themes – empiricism, sociologism, naturalism, scientism and social reformism. He was not, however, unequivocal in his admiration of Comte (Lukes, 1973). In particular, although subscribing to naturalism, he did not do so dogmatically. Like Mill earlier, he thought that Comte's formulation of the unity of the sciences in terms of the law of three stages verged on metaphysical speculation. Only extensive and rigorous empirical inquiry, which Comte had not undertaken, could establish whether or not such an all-embracing law were true, and whether naturalism were viable (Durkheim and Fauconnet, 1903).

What is significant about Durkheim in connection with understandings of 'positivism' is that he added to Comte's abstract philosophical themes another, quite independent tradition, that of statistics. In some of his works – most notably in his book *Suicide* (1897) – Durkheim brought together nineteenth-century Comtean social philosophy and the collection and analysis of quantified social facts. That *Suicide* is commonly identified as the classic example of the positivist study of society testifies to the prevalence of another conception of positivism in sociology: positivism$_6$ is a theory of knowledge according to which the natural science of sociology consists of the collection and statistical analysis of quantitative data about society.

This brief outline of nineteenth-century positive systems and their early twentieth-century developments should not lead one to forget that there were many more actors on the intellectual stage than there has been space to mention. None of the six positivisms was either the dominant philosophical movement from the mid-nineteenth to the early twentieth century, or without rivals as a general orientation to the study of society. In philosophy there was in the 1890s a 'revolt against positivism' (Hughes, 1958) which swept even Britain, the bastion of empiricism. It took the form of a resurgence of idealism and romanticism, vehemently opposed to empiricism and naturalism. The human world, it proclaimed, is quite different from the natural world, being pervaded by meanings which must be studied in ways remote from those applicable in the sciences of nature (Outhwaite, 1975). In sociology there was at the beginning of the twentieth century in Britain and America a revolt against system-building, against very general theories of historical change, motivated partly by the growing distaste for Spencerian sociology, with governments seeking to introduce social reforms aimed at mitigating the deleterious effects of capitalism. Sociology became involved in documenting practical social problems and applying anthropological techniques to modern societies, as in the urban ethnographies of the Chicago school in America and social surveys and community studies in Britain. In France, after Durkheim's death in 1917, sociology drifted towards extreme generalities on the one hand and ethnographic field work on the other (Hawthorne, 1976). In Germany high-level disputes over the proper nature of sociology, history and economics continued alongside large-scale surveys organised to collect information about current social problems. Throughout German-speaking Europe Marxism became a serious candidate for the natural science of society. Considered as a general materialist theory of the economic development of capitalist society, it was widely debated as an alternative to the French sociologistic and Anglo-American individualistic theories of progress (Bottomore, 1979), though even many social reformers found its revolutionary projections alarming.

This sketch of the period is, of course, oversimplified, but it does indicate that Comtean concerns were not simply carried through into twentieth-century sociology and philosophy unimpeded and undiluted by other social and intellectual movements. Against the rich variety of the period since his death, Comte's sociological legacy is threefold. First, in reaction to his religion of humanity (positivism$_4$) there is now little sympathy for the idea that sociology might provide a secular alternative to established religions or other belief systems as an integrative social force. Secondly, in reaction to Spencer's individualistic evolutionism and its eugenicist extension (positivism$_5$) there was for a long period in the early and mid-twentieth century a rejection of grand theories of individual and social progress. This was accompanied by a shift in focus to the analysis of functional relations between social items rather than their sequential development, from what Comte had called social dynamics, the study of the historical progression of types of society, to social statics, the analysis of synchronic relations between social institutions. Where general theories of development have now returned to favour, they have been less influenced by Comte's theory of history (positivism$_1$) than by other traditions, especially Marxism. Lastly, Comte's naturalism (positivism$_3$) has been fused with statistics, with the result that the natural scientific study of society is now commonly considered to involve the production and test of social laws by the collection and manipulation of quantified social facts (positivism$_6$). Comte made no contribution to this statistical tradition; indeed he was quite opposed to it. The origin and development of this alternative and independent root of positivism is the subject of the next chapter. Comte's philosophical legacy (positivism$_2$) has largely been absorbed into the general background to newer twentieth-century conceptions of positivist philosophy, which are explored in subsequent chapters.

2
Statistics

The history of statistics is not the history of one tradition but of several, for the term 'statistics' has been used to refer to several different ideas (Walker, 1929; Westergaard, 1932; Hacking, 1975). One important distinction is between descriptive statistics and inductive statistics. The former refers to the measurement and enumeration of the characteristics of populations of people, property, institutions, and so on, and the latter (also called theoretical or probability statistics) refers to methods used to infer from information about a sample to information about the population from which the sample is drawn. Confusingly (following Fisher, 1925), the information about the sample is sometimes referred to as the sample statistic, as contrasted with the population parameter, which is the analogous information about the population. Another important distinction is between descriptive statistics and explanatory (or relational) statistics, though because descriptive here has a different sense than before, this second distinction is better labelled univariate versus multivariate statistics (where multivariate includes bivariate as the simplest case). The former refers to measures of the distribution of the members of some sample or population over each of their characteristics taken one at a time, and the latter refers to measures of the distribution of conjunctions of characteristics of the members of some sample or population. Combining these distinctions gives the four possibilities displayed in Table 2.1, which also lists some examples of what is meant by each combination.

Table 2.1   *Branches of Statistics*

	descriptive	inductive or theoretical or probability
univariate *or* *'descriptive'*	frequency distributions central tendency dispersion index numbers	interval estimates hypothesis tests
multivariate *(including bivariate)* *or* *explanatory* *or* *relational*	measures of covariation measures of agreement cluster analysis factor analysis	interval estimates hypothesis tests analysis of variance

These four branches of statistics have not always been distinct either in their historical development or in ahistorical reviews of them as sets of techniques. Nevertheless, some attempt will be made to separate them in the following discussion.

DESCRIPTIVE SOCIAL STATISTICS

The practice of counting and recording characteristics of the population and material resources goes back to Antiquity, but received new impetus in the early seventeenth century, a period of rapid socioeconomic change, with the spread of merchant capitalism and its spirit of systematic empirical inquiry (Lazarsfeld, 1961; Shaw and Miles, 1979). Demographic and economic facts about the population and about trade were seen as essential aids for formulating government policy, for example, for determining the people and provisions available for the military, for constructing a tax system based on individual members of the population rather than on land or housing, for estimating the cost of poor relief, and for calculating the value of annuities, which were a common method of state fundraising. Vital statistics, describing the principal events in the lives of people, such as baptism and burial, had begun to be recorded in the registers of parish churches in Britain and France in the sixteenth century. The Englishman William Petty (1623–87) introduced the term 'political arithmetic' to describe systematic reasoning about such population statistics, the idea being that a science of society based on the supposedly neutral numerical information would be free from political bias and opinion (Buck, 1977). It was Petty's friend John Graunt (1620–74) who provided the first example of political arithmetic. Because of public interest in the ravages of the plague, from 1603 the City of London published weekly listings of christenings and burials, with deaths classified according to disease, but without recording the age at death. In his work *Natural and Political Observations . . . made upon the Bills of Mortality*, published in 1662, Graunt examined such matters as the variation in the incidence of diseases over time and the effects of the plague on birth rates and upon emigration from London to the country, and he ingeniously estimated the proportion of people dying at various ages, the life expectancies of people of a given age and the population of London.

The work of the political arithmeticians did not take the name 'statistics' until late in the eighteenth century. 'Stateistics' was initially used to describe the activity, that began in mid-seventeenth-century Germany, of cataloguing features of the many states, principalities and free cities that made up that country. Statistics was widely taught in German universities as an aid to statecraft. Complicated sets of categories were devised. Initially the detail that went into the classificatory schema consisted of verbal descriptions of such matters as the land, constitution and administration of each state, or of references to sources of information on these matters. By the end of the eighteenth century, to facilitate comparisons, tables were being produced with the states along one edge and the categories down another, and the verbal entries replaced by numbers, a development derogated as vulgar 'table statistics' by the teachers of the earlier statecraft.

Nevertheless, it was the table statisticians and political arithmeticians who usurped the name 'statistics', and the socioeconomic changes accompanying the advent of industrial capitalism brought renewed interest in their type of systematic collection and analysis of economic and vital statistics in early nineteenth-century Britain and France and late nineteenth-century Germany and America. Again the purpose was to aid policy formation. Social reformers among the new bourgeoisie, concerned about the fate of the urbanised industrial working class and about their own position in society, formed statistical societies, organised large-scale systematic social surveys and published journals, all to support their demands for the reforms they believed would stabilise society (Oberschall, 1972a; Shaw and Miles, 1979). Numerical information on a wider and wider range of topics was collected, and the Parisian lawyer André Michel Guerry coined the term 'moral statistics' as the analogue of vital statistics to describe quantified measures of the depravity of the masses – crime, imprisonment, intemperence, sexual conduct, public health, schooling, and so on (P. Abrams, 1968). In England the centralised state agencies that Petty had earlier campaigned for were finally established: the Statistical Department of the Board of Trade for economic statistics in 1832 and the General Register Office for civil registration of vital statistics in 1836. Other European countries followed suit during the nineteenth century, and national decennial censuses were instituted over the same period.

What intrigued the statisticians was the regularity of the phenomena whose occurrence they recorded. (For example, the ratio of male to female births was constant over time.) Such stability, the statisticians mistakenly argued, could not be due to chance. Instead they suggested, first, that it was determined by divine design, and later, that it was the result of some common natural cause (Hacking, 1975, ch. 18). This idea of underlying causes was reinforced by the formalisation of the mathematical expression for the 'law of error' – now called the normal curve – by Abraham De Moivre (1667–1754), and its application to astronomical observations as a theory of measurement error by the Parisian Pierre Simon de Laplace (1749–1827) and the German Carl Friedrich Gauss (1777–1855). They maintained that the characteristic bell-shaped frequency distribution of measurements is due to the operation of a multitude of accidental causes, whereas the 'true' value is represented by the mean, which is determined by a constant cause (or perhaps by a time-dependent variable cause). The analogue was the distribution of arrows on a target: all were aimed at the bull's eye, but breezes, irregularities in the arrows, and so on, caused them to be dispersed around the centre. What was of interest was the bull's eye, not the distribution due to the interference of minor factors, dismissed as errors. The practical problem was how to discount the errors and estimate the true value underlying the distribution. The solution, the astronomers assumed, was to collect a long run of observations of one body, or observations from a large number of bodies, and average them. In this way causal sequences between true values represented by the means could be isolated. Applying this to astronomical observations enabled them to demonstrate the universal applicability of Newton's laws to the motions of heavenly bodies.

When the Belgian astronomer Adolphe Quételet (1796–1874) found that the height of human beings was also distributed according to the law of error, he realised that Laplace's idea might have wider applicability than astronomy. He proposed that the regularities exhibited by both vital and moral statistics are the result of common causes and that irregularities are 'errors' resulting from the operation of a multitude of accidental causes. In his book *Sur l'homme et le développement de ses facultés, ou essai de physique sociale*, published in 1835, he introduced his famous tool of analysis *l'homme moyen* (the typical or average man), a measure of the 'true value' of the condition of society from which was excluded the 'errors' arising from peculiarities of the individuals composing it. Around this notion he sought to construct an empirical science of society, the study of moral or social facts and the social conditions that caused them. For example, he analysed crime rates, and the effects of sex, education, climate and the seasons on them.

Yet, in general, Quételet and the other administrators and reformers responsible for gathering descriptive social statistics during the nineteenth century limited themselves to immediate practical concerns, and did not construct general theories of history about the social processes they documented so comprehensively (Glazer, 1959). Conversely, the social philosophers like Comte and Spencer, if they used evidence at all, relied on comparative and historical methods in which qualitative material from historical and anthropological sources was used to arrange societies in an order of progression. The gulf between them was great. Indeed, it was Quételet's use of 'social physics' to describe his statistical science that led Comte to abandon that term in favour of 'sociology' in an effort to distance his highest positive science from mere statistics (Comte, 1877, p. 15). And Durkheim criticised Quételet's notion of the average man as being an inadequate indicator of social forces, because it confused the average of the properties of society's component individuals with the emergent properties of the collectivity (Durkheim, 1897, p. 300). Nevertheless, it was Durkheim who brought together Comte's sociology and descriptive social statistics and so established that sixth conception of positivism already mentioned in the last chapter: the collection and statistical analysis of quantitative information about society.

MULTIVARIATE STATISTICS

Although it was quite common for political arithmeticians and moral statisticians to compare measures of different aspects of society and offer explanations of one in terms of the others, it was the British eugenicists who formalised procedures of bivariate and multivariate analysis. Galton, writing when social Darwinism was a powerful influence, understood the normal curve quite differently from Quételet (Hilts, 1973). For Quételet it was a law of error, for Galton a law of distribution. Instead of considering that the variations of human characteristics were due to accidental causes or measurement errors whose influence was to be eradicated by averaging over populations, Galton's interest, first sketched out in two articles in *Macmillan's Magazine* in 1865, was in explaining the variability of the characteristics. In particular, he wanted to demonstrate that (at least a fraction of) the normal distribution of the characteristics of populations of biological organisms is the result of a single cause – heredity – and not a multitude of accidental causes. He argued that if the variability among each generation of offspring were normally distributed as a result of accidental causes, then the overall variability of the population would increase from generation to generation. Since the observed intergenerational variability does not increase then there must be some factor – inheritance – that reduces family variability and causes reversion to the mean for that family line of descent. To establish his case, Galton first bred sweet peas, raised moths and studied hounds, but later, by offering prizes for 'records of family faculties', collected sufficient anthropological information on generations of families to be able to investigate directly questions of human inheritance.

Galton introduced the coefficient of reversion, symbolised by r and later renamed the coefficient of regression, in an attempt to measure the degree to which a child inherits the characteristics of its parents (Walker, 1929, ch. 5). This soon led him to the notion of the co-relation coefficient, or as he renamed it, the correlation coefficient, to measure the strength of the relationship between two characteristics. These notions of regression and correlation became widely known after the publication of Galton's book *Natural Inheritance* in 1889. They were refined and extended in the 1890s by Pearson, who held the chair of applied mathematics and mechanics at University College, London, from 1884, where he formed the Department of Applied Statistics in 1911 (Pearson, 1938). Pearson took Galton's work to show that mathematics need not be restricted to natural phenomena and relations of causality between them for causality was only the limit of the broader notion of correlation, which made human phenomena available to mathematical treatment. Especially in his arguments with the Mendelians and environmentalists about the origin and nature of the generational variations in biological organisms that are central to Darwin's theory of evolution and to the eugenicist programme (MacKenzie and Barnes, 1979), Pearson developed Galton's work by introducing, *inter alia*, the ideas of multiple, partial, biserial and tetrachoric correlation, curvilinear regression and the chi-square test, as well as giving the modern name to many other statistical ideas such as the mode, kurtosis, standard deviation, and homo- and hetero-scedasticity (Dudycha and Dudycha, 1972). Pearson's and his students' techniques provided the formal tools with which to test empirically hypotheses about the relationships between social variables, relationships which otherwise could only be investigated in an informal way, as in the work of the nineteenth-century moral statisticians, and as exemplified by Durkheim's *Suicide* (1897).

INDUCTIVE STATISTICS

Probability theory or the calculus of chances is the mathematical formulation of the *expected* regularities in (or distribution of frequencies of) events, and has its roots in the analysis of games of chance – cards and dice. The first book on probability theory was the posthumously published *Ars Conjectandi* (1713) by the Swiss mathematician Jacques Bernoulli (1654–1705). Descriptive statistics is the study of *observed* uni-, bi-, or multivariate regularities in (or distribution of frequencies of) various characteristics of aggregates. Although there had previously been contact between the two, they were brought together most fruitfully from the time of Galton. Because the empirical work of eugenicists, biologists and zoologists involved samples of plants, animals and humans, whereas they wanted empirical justification for their claims about whole species or populations, their work on bi- and multivariate correlation also, necessarily, involved the development of inductive statistics. They had to formulate and test not only substantive hypotheses about the relations between different characteristics of the objects in their samples, but also statistical hypotheses (which are less misleadingly described as generalisability hypotheses) about the relations between their findings for samples and what was true of the populations from which the samples were drawn. For example, given some particular evidence about the characteristics of a sample, the question arises: what is the probability, or what confidence can we have, that the characteristics are possessed by the population as a whole, and are not merely specific to the particular sample chosen?

This question can only be answered when the expected regularities in sample characteristics are known, that is, when it is known how often one would expect to get (what probability there is of getting) a certain measure of a characteristic in a sample if one drew all possible samples of a given size from the population. Such a distribution of probabilities, known as a sampling distribution, is a theoretical distribution, mathematically derived from assumptions about both the population and the sampling procedure used. It would be empirically observed only if one drew all the samples of the given size and measured the characteristics in each of them, but that is precisely what the researchers wanted to avoid, as their aim was to generalise from one sample to the population. (Nevertheless, it is true that some sampling distributions were obtained empirically.)

The first sampling distribution to be made use of was the normal curve, for it was found that the means of different large samples (say, greater than 100) drawn by simple random sampling methods from the same population followed a normal distribution. (In simple random sampling, each possible sample of a given size has an equal

chance of being selected from the population.) It therefore
became possible, given the known mathematical properties
of the normal curve, to state the probability with which a
fixed interval around the sample mean will include the
population mean. For example there is a 95% probability
that the interval bounded by 1·96 standard deviations
around the sample mean will contain the population mean.
(The standard deviation is a measure of dispersion and is
defined as the square root of the sum of the squared deviations from the sample mean divided by the sample size.)
The use of the normal curve here, as a sampling distribution in inductive statistics, is quite different from its use (in
the early nineteenth century) by astronomers as a description of the observed distribution of a large number of
measurements of a particular characteristic around its
'true' value and as a basis, therefore, for calculating some
standardised measure of their dispersion, such as the misleadingly named probable error, which is the width of the
band under the normal curve that contains 50% of the
measurements, and which has now largely been replaced
by the standard deviation.

The general problem at the beginning of the twentieth
century became one of deriving sampling distributions of
other descriptive statistical measures, especially the new
correlation measures, so that estimates of the association
of population characteristics could be made from observations on samples. Notable advances were made in
the 1920s and 1930s by William Sealy Gosset (1876–1937)
while working as a brewer for Guinness in Dublin,
involved both in relating ingredients to the quality of the
brew they produced and in barley-breeding experiments,
and by Ronald Aylmer Fisher (1890–1962), chief stat-
istician at the Rothamsted Agricultural Station before
taking up the headship of the Department of Eugenics at
University College, London, in 1933, after Pearson's
retirement. Gosset, who wrote under the name Student (of
Student's t) and who had a year in London working with
Pearson, raised the problem that the sampling distributions of small random samples are non-normal, and Fisher

then determined exact sampling distributions for a wide variety of correlation measures for small samples, and also laid the basis for analysis of variance. Their work extended the applicability of statistical inference from large samples collected from natural populations to the results of small-scale controlled experiments. These experiments were initially on plant-breeding, but subsequently came to dominate psychology.

THE STATISTICAL SCIENCE OF SOCIETY

The development of multivariate and inductive statistics made possible a radical change in the nature of social surveys, though even in Britain, where the statistical advances were first made, the implications for social research were slow to be absorbed (Selvin, 1976). The first phase of privately sponsored British surveys had faded away by the mid-nineteenth century for a number of reasons: because the social reformers who had instigated them achieved the reformist legislation they had sought; because a period of economic prosperity made the problems of the proletariat less pressing; and because of the increasing influence of social Darwinism with its anti-reformist spirit. But a second phase began during the economic depression at the end of the century (M. Abrams, 1951, ch. 4). In response to what he took to be exaggerations about the extent of poverty made by the leaders of the nascent socialist movement, the Liverpool shipowner Charles Booth (1840–1916) organised his famous survey of the London poor, beginning work in 1886 and collecting his results together in the seventeen-volume *Life and Labour of the People of London* (1902–3). Booth's work, like the earlier social surveys, was largely descriptive, and was aimed at social reforms to stabilise society. He did not use any of the new relational statistics. To assess the 'causes of poverty' he simply compared the percentage who were poor due to questions of employment (lack of work or low pay), due to questions of habit (idleness, drunkenness, or thriftlessness) and due to circumstances (sickness or large families) and, contrary to popular opinion, he found that far fewer suffered poverty as a result of 'habit' than as a result of (un)employment (Booth, 1902–3, Vol. 1, pp. 146–9). It was one of Pearson's students, George Udny Yule (1871–1951), who first applied the newly developed multivariate regression and correlation techniques to social data (as opposed to agricultural, biological, or psychological data) in a secondary analysis of some of Booth's survey data, the results of which led him to challenge Booth's claim that these data demonstrated that there is no relation between out-of-doors poor relief and the percentage of pauperism (Yule, 1895).

Wanting to discover the full extent of poverty, Booth attempted to survey the whole of the London population. His primary source of information was school board visitors, who visited every house and had detailed knowledge of the living conditions of the parents of pre-school and school-age children. But because these parents are not a random sample of all adults, Booth could not have supported his conclusions about the whole population by deploying the sort of inductive statistics that were becoming available, even had he wished to. In order to generalise to the whole population, he had to make assumptions about the proportion of men without children in each of his categories of poverty and of employment, and of the number of post-school children and young persons (aged 13–20) in each household (Booth, 1902–3, Vol. 1, pp. 4–5).

'Representative investigations' had been discussed by the International Statistical Association in the 1890s, and some form of sampling had been used on various surveys in the nineteenth century (Seng, 1951; S. Cole, 1972), but the first random sample survey was not undertaken until 1912, when Arthur Lyon Bowley (1869–1957), who became the first professor of statistics at the London School of Economics in 1915, organised a study of Reading (Bowley, 1913). He followed this with others in Northampton, Warrington, Stanley and Bolton, publishing the results together in *Livelihood and Poverty* in 1915. After that the use of random sampling in social surveys gradually spread (Stephan, 1948), further developments being made when Jerzy Neyman (1894–) criticised purposive selection (or quota sampling) and provided the theoretical basis for stratified sampling (Neyman, 1934). A check on the reliability of results from random samples in social research came in 1941 in the report by B. Seebohm Rowntree (1871–1954) on his second survey of York, conducted in 1935 and published as *Poverty and Progress* in 1941. As in his first, 1901, York survey, Rowntree attempted again in 1935 to interview all wage-earners. But in his report he included a chapter where he simulated samples by analysing one in ten, one in twenty, and so on, up to one in fifty of the completed schedules, from which he concluded that sampling could provide reliable results. Even so, in the third study of York in 1950 he again attempted a complete coverage rather than taking a sample (Rowntree and Lavers, 1951).

Explanatory random sample social surveys of the kind whose description now forms the core of many sociological research methods texts did not become routine in Britain until after the Second World War, when they gained respectability from their widespread use in America. In the early twentieth century the largely British developments in multivariate and inductive statistics that provide the rationale for this type of survey were tainted by their association with the eugenics movement, which was opposed by those responsible for the institutionalisation of academic sociology. L. T. Hobhouse (1864–1929), for example, who was appointed to the first British chair of sociology in 1907 (the Martin White Professorship at the London School of Economics), objected strongly to attempts by the eugenicists to reduce the science of society to part of the science of biology (Collini, 1979). In Germany the Verein für Sozialpolitik (Association for Social Policy), founded in 1872 by university economists, civil servants and others, organised nationwide surveys on the agrarian problems that arose after unification in 1871, as the peasantry was displaced by rural wage labour, and on industrial workers following the successes of the socialists at the polls in the post-Bismarck 1890s. (Max Weber, 1864–1920, was an active member from 1888 until his death: Lazarsfeld and Oberschall, 1965.) But the Verein's members were mainly preoccupied with legislating for social reforms and disputing philosophical issues like free will versus determinism (Oberschall, 1965), and consequently their data collection was unsystematic and their analyses were indifferent by today's standards. In France the Durkheimian synthesis gradually dissolved after Durkheim's death in 1917. But a similar synthesis, between statistics and nineteenth-century cosmology, this time in its Spencerian individualistic guise rather than its Comtean sociologistic one, became firmly established in America. There, the men who headed the new sociology departments that were founded during the rapid expansion of universities at the end of the nineteenth century realised that academic acceptability depended upon leaving behind the spirit of liberal reformism that had inspired the creation of their departments, and demonstrating instead that their discipline was scientific (Walker, 1929, ch. 7). This was particularly the case with Franklin Giddings (1855–1931), who held the chair at Columbia University from 1894. He was influenced by Comte, Spencer, Durkheim and Pearson, and most notably by Mill. In his writings he argued for a sociology that closely followed Mill's methods (see Chapter 5), and he gave statistical analysis of precisely measured social facts a central place in science. Under his headship Columbia became the centre for training in the rigorous application of quantitative methods to sociological issues. Columbia students such as William Fielding Ogburn (1886–1959) and F. Stuart Chapin (1888–1978) – who learned the new statistics from the Columbia econometrician H. L. Moore, who frequently visited Galton and Pearson in London – were instrumental in professionalising American sociology around survey research and statistics of all types (Martindale, 1961; Oberschall, 1972b; Hawthorne, 1976). Statistics were used to provide both the methods of inquiry to legitimate the scientific status of sociology and the standards of scholarship to exclude the propagators of unsystematic generalities in the nineteenth-century tradition of social philosophy (C. C. Taylor, 1920). This professionalism reached a peak in the studies of the American army undertaken by a team of behavioural scientists during the Second World War under the direction of Samuel Stouffer (1900–60), a student of Ogburn's who had worked with Pearson and Fisher in London for a year. The results were published in four volumes, of which the two-volume *The American Soldier* is the best known (Stouffer *et al.*, 1949a, 1949b).

The natural science of society, these new professionals maintained, would be value-neutral if emotion and prejudice were disciplined by the dispassionate and meticulous application of statistical techniques to objective numerical data. But this aspiration, that statistics would provide the foundation of a value-free science of society, has constantly failed because the use of statistics in social inquiry and with it the sixth conception of positivism have never been without controversy. All types of statistics have been challenged from a wide variety of standpoints that range from technical quibbles to epistemological quarrels.

The descriptive adequacy of social statistics, especially official statistics gathered by government agencies, has been found wanting because of measurement errors, which for some pose technical issues of estimating validity and reliability (Zeller and Carmines, 1980), but for others, especially sociologists influenced by ordinary language philosophy, undermine the empiricist conception of language upon which quantitative description is said to rely (Winch, 1958; Phillips, 1973).

The appropriateness of multivariate statistics has been questioned because, until the 1950s, it was only for interval-level data that measures of covariation were well developed (other than chi-square for nominal data) whereas, it was argued, most sociological data are ordinal. Some maintain that this question has been answered by technical developments both in scaling ordinal data, that is, mapping it on to interval measures such as Lickert and Thurstone scales (Upshaw, 1968), and in devising an extensive family of ordinal-level covariation measures (Siegel, 1956). Others argue that the question raises fundamental issues about the nature of causal relations in the human sciences (Levison, 1974; Davidson, 1980), issues that are left untouched (or whose solutions are presupposed) by sociologists' attempts to infer causality from observed correlations in non-experimental data through the introduction of causal or path-analytic models (Blalock, 1964; Boudon, 1968).

The application of inductive statistics as a means of generalising sample data has been controversial for a number of reasons. An early argument was about the form that interval estimation should take. It was, essentially, an argument about the meaning of probability statements. In 1930 Fisher proposed that on the basis of observations on a random sample and a known sampling distribution, one could calculate a permissible range for a population parameter, that is, the probability that the parameter lay within the bounds of what he called a fiducial interval of a given magnitude (Fisher, 1930). Neyman, attempting to clarify this notion, maintained that whether or not a parameter is in a given interval is not a probability in the accepted sense, since the parameter either is in the interval (probability = 1) or is not (probability = 0). The probability is associated, instead, with the confidence interval (as Neyman called it): it is the probability that the interval derived from the sample contains the population parameter (Neyman, 1937). Fisher bitterly disputed this and continued to extend his own idea, though Neyman's notion came to prevail.

Interval estimation was overtaken in popularity after the Second World War, however, by hypothesis-testing, especially in psychology and sociology. In this approach one explicitly tests a statistical hypothesis, called the null hypothesis, usually (but not necessarily) that chance generated the sample findings (in the sense that although measures on the sample support the substantive research hypothesis, that finding is peculiar to the particular sample and is not true of the population), against the alternative statistical hypothesis that the substantive research hypothesis supported by the sample findings *can* be generalised to the population (Blalock, 1960). To do this one derives a distribution of some feature of all samples of the chosen size on the basis of assumptions about the sampling method (for example, that it is random) and about the population (for example, that its properties of interest are normally distributed and that the null hypothesis is true of it). The appropriate feature of the observed sample (called the test statistic) is then compared with this sampling distribution to see how rare the sample is. If there is a low probability of that kind of sample being selected, say, less than α in a 100 chance (where α is commonly 5, 1, or 0·1), then the null hypothesis can be rejected and the alternative hypothesis accepted, provided that the other assumptions hold true. The finding described by the alternative hypothesis is said to be statistically significant at the $\alpha \%$ level, which means that on the evidence of the sample findings about the substantive hypothesis and given the truth of the assumptions, there is less than $\alpha \%$ probability that the null hypothesis has been rejected when it is in fact true. The significance level α is the probability of taking the sample findings to indicate or signify that the substantive research hypothesis is true of the population when it is in fact peculiar to the sample. This mistake is called Type I error. It has to be balanced against the probability of failing to reject the null hypothesis when it is false, which is called Type II error. Where one decides the balance should lie might depend, for example, on whether it is more important to risk convicting the innocent or to risk acquitting the guilty, or whether it is preferable to risk rejecting what should be accepted or to risk accepting what should be rejected.

Doubts arise about significance tests when they are unthinkingly generated by computer package programs and employed by the statistically inept. Common mistakes are confusing a statistically significant result (one where there is a high probability that the correct decision has been made in generalising the sample finding to the population) with a substantively significant one (one that is theoretically tenable or has important practical consequences); confusing the level of significance with the strength of relationship; distorting the reporting of results by publishing only statistically significant ones; failing to take account of the power of statistical tests, which is the probability of accepting the alternative hypothesis when it is true; forgetting that there are sources of error other than sampling; and employing statistical tests when the data are about the whole population and not about a sample (Sterling, 1959; Galtung, 1967, pp. 358–89; Morrison and Henkel, 1970; Atkins and Jarrett, 1979). Such problems as these might be overcome by more careful and informed use of significance tests, or by using confidence intervals instead. But both these techniques for generalising from social data gathered from samples have been subject to the more fundamental criticism that the underlying assumptions that have to be made about the sampling method and population cannot be met in social research. Again, for some these are technical issues that have been solved by the development of statistical tests that do not rely on specifying the exact form of the population (sometimes misleadingly called distribution-free or non-parametric statistics: Siegel, 1956), by advances in sampling theory (Lazerwitz, 1968), and by the development of test statistics for non-random samples (for example, for matched pairs). For others, they indicate that technical devices like probability calculus cannot solve the fundamental problem of induction, that is, the problem of justifying statements about the population on the basis of empirical information about a sample.

In sum: among the supporters of positivism[6], the difficulties involved in extending descriptive, multivariate and inductive statistics to social research are merely technical ones, and considerable advances have been made, and will continue to be made, in resolving them. Among critics, however, the difficulties are indicators of major epistemological problems with empiricism, causality and induction in sociology. In the following chapters, therefore, I return to the philosophy of positivism to explore these epistemological issues further.

3

Logical Positivism

Comte's philosophical legacy remains only as part of the rich nineteenth-century sediment out of which grew twentieth-century developments in philosophy, particularly the remarkably revitalised form of positivism that appeared in the 1920s and 1930s in the works of the Vienna Circle. The most prominent members of this circle, who met in a seminar directed by Moritz Schlick (1882–1936), professor in the philosophy of inductive sciences at the University of Vienna, were Rudolf Carnap (1891–1970), Herbert Feigl (1902–), Hans Hahn (1879–1934), Viktor Kraft (1880–1975), Otto Neurath (1882–1945) and Friedrich Waismann (1896–1959). Like Comte a century before, members of the circle, especially Neurath and the frequent visitor Philipp Frank (1884–1966), worked at least initially for a new era of enlightenment, motivated by the scientistic concern to make all disciplines truly scientific so that they would provide the basis for rational action and thereby avoid a repetition of recent social disorganisation, in this case the disaster of the First World War. But they broke with those nineteenth-century conceptions of positivism which consisted of reflecting upon the general human condition and producing theories of history, directives of social progress. That is, they broke with positivism$_1$ and positivism$_5$. The Vienna Circle took to heart what G. E. Moore (1873–1958) in his *Principia Ethica* (1903) called the naturalistic fallacy, that it is fallacious to argue from what science tells us is the case to what ought to be, that it is impossible to deduce what is morally desirable from scientific knowledge of the facts. Morality, the Vienna Circle believed, is a matter of intuition or taste, untouched by science. Science tells us only what will happen, given certain conditions. It cannot tell us what should happen. The Vienna Circle's positivism was scientistic but not progressivist or social reformist. They believed that the growth of science would benefit humankind, but not that it would do so necessarily. They were naturalistic, believing that all sciences could be unified because they took the same form, but unlike Comte and Spencer, they excluded morality from the sciences.

The Vienna Circle sought to highlight the ways in which their positivism differed from nineteenth-century positivist philosophy by giving their programme the name 'logical positivism'. (This term first appeared in Blumberg and Feigl, 1931.) In their manifesto issued in 1929 they stressed the centrality to their ideas (then described as 'the scientific conception of the world') of two characteristics:

> *First* it is *empiricist and positivist*: there is knowledge only from experience, which rests on what is immediately given. This sets the limit for the content of legitimate science. *Second*, the scientific world-conception is marked by application of a certain method, namely *logical analysis*. The aim of scientific effort is to reach the goal, unified science, by applying logical analysis to the empirical material. (Neurath, Hahn and Carnap, 1929, p. 11; emphasis in the original)

LOGIC

There had always been a dilemma about logic, the study of argument and sound reasoning: was its topic the human activity of inferring or the formal relationship of implying? The former, empiricist interpretation gives logic a place among the empirical sciences at the expense of making its statements susceptible to empirical refutation, while the latter, rationalist interpretation captures the inviolability of logic at the expense of rendering its statements beyond experience and therefore dangerously metaphysical in the eyes of positivists. Traditional British empiricists such as John Locke (1632–1704) and David Hume (1711–76) recognised the possibility of both interpretations but had little use for formal logic. For them, logic was the study of human understanding, a branch of empirical psychology that explores the ways in which knowledge is inferred from experience. Formal logic (which up to the beginning of the nineteenth century was still largely confined to Aristotle's syllogisms) merely provided formulae for manipulating ideas, and was silent on the issue, crucial to empiricists, of the relationship between those ideas and experience. J. S. Mill developed to its extreme this traditional empiricist approach. All logic to him was the study of human infer- ences, of the practical inductive procedures through which empirical data is systematically organised by the human psyche to produce scientific laws. For Mill, even the pro- positions of formal logic, and with it pure mathematics, were generalisations of experience. But experience is a shaky basis on which to found the certainties of logic, and Mill's arguments in support of his view were found wanting, as will be seen when considering induction in Chapter 5.

A solution to the dilemma about the status of logic became available through developments in formal logic from the middle of the nineteenth century onwards. Syllo- gistic logic had been easy to criticise because, being restricted to propositions expressed in subject-predicate form, its applicability to the analysis of ordinary argu- ments and reasoning was very limited. This deficiency was overcome by reconceiving logic as the analysis of the properties of different sorts of relations, in addition to the 'is' and 'are' of syllogisms' propositions (Passmore, 1957, ch. 9). Correspondingly, as the emphasis shifted to rela- tions, the specific ideas entertained by reason (that is, the subject matter of reasoning) lost importance, and the content of the related propositions could be represented by abstract uninterpreted symbols. Logic was reformulated in algebraic terms, as the formal analysis of implication relations between variables, expressed in context-and content-free propositions.

The new logics provided ideal languages in which the meanings of the operators or logical connectives relating variables were precisely defined (rather like the $+$, $-$, etc., of algebra). Logic became a set of formal syntactical rules for constructing compound propositions out of elementary propositions or variables. These rules specified how the truth or falsity of compound propositions should be calculated from the truth or falsity of their constituent elementary propositions. Applying these rules shows that within an ideal language, some statements are necessarily true and some are necessarily false solely by virtue of the meanings of the logical connectives they contain, irrespective of the truth or falsity of the elementary propositions connected, just as $2 + 2 = 4$ is true and $3 - 1 = 4$ is false irrespective of whether they refer to numbers of pins, pounds, or people. These statements are either tautologies, such as $p \vee -p$ ('p or not-p') which is logically true no matter whether p is empirically true or false, or self-contradictions such as p & $-p$ ('p and not-p') which is logically false no matter whether p is empirically true or false. Tautologies and self-contradictions are, then, vacuous propositions that give no information about the world, for they are true or false (respectively) independent of whether or not p correctly describes the way things are in the world. Their truth or falsity is established by analysis of logical connectives rather than by investigation of the empirical world. They are analytically, not empirically, true or false.

Establishing that formal logic does not mysteriously encapsulate fundamental empirical truths, but instead precisely explicates conceptual relations within symbol systems devoid of empirical content, made it acceptable to empiricists, for logic so conceived is not beyond experience in the way that metaphysics is. This conception of logic also suggested a solution to the longstanding debate between empiricists and rationalists about the source of the certainty, generality and objectivity of mathematical truths. Nineteenth-century developments such as non-

Euclidean geometries and transfinite numbers violated experiences of spatial relationships and of counting things, and made Mill's radical empiricist suggestion that mathematical propositions are generalisations of experience increasingly untenable. But instead of returning to the rationalist view, that mathematical propositions are true because they reflect the way in which our minds work and cannot be false because our minds cannot work in any other way, a new logicist conception of mathematics began to gain strength. This new view agreed with rationalism against empiricism that mathematical truths, like logical truths, are *a priori* (that is, their truth can be known without reference to experience) but it maintained that they are *a priori* because they are analytic, because they tell us nothing about experience. This idea was prompted by the achievement of the Italian Giuseppe Peano (1858–1932) and his colleagues who had succeeded in deriving arithmetic from a small set of premisses. It was consolidated in the work of the German mathematician Gottlob Frege (1848–1925) and culminated in the *Principia Mathematica* (1910–13), the three-volume work by Bertrand Russell (1872–1970) and Alfred Whitehead (1861–1947). In this work Russell and Whitehead formulated a new logic of relations and then, using the clearly defined rules of this logic, attempted to show that the whole of mathematics could be constructed, in a series of precise steps, from a small number of primitives and axiomatic definitions. If this were possible, then it would become clear that the truths of mathematics are neither induced from experience (in which case mathematical statements would be laws of nature) nor deduced from innate ideas of reason (in which case mathematical statements would be laws of the mind) but are tautological and analytic. That is, their truth is established by applying the rules of the *Principia* logic to the definitions they contain, and they say nothing about the world.

That Russell and Whitehead's attempt, though highly ingenious, was ultimately unsuccessful is now generally agreed, but the *Principia* was a crucial resource for the

Vienna Circle (Carnap, 1930). For what it suggested was that traditional philosophical problems could be resolved by application of the new logic. Logical analysis would sweep away previous philosophical paradoxes, just as it had resolved the longstanding debate between rationalists and empiricists about the status of mathematical truths. This logicistic approach became a characteristic of the Vienna Circle: issues were to be investigated by reconstructing them in a formal language, which clarifies the relations between the sets of propositions that constitute the issues. The consequences this approach had for the Vienna Circle's analysis of scientific knowledge will become clear after reviewing their ideas about empiricism.

EMPIRICISM

Empiricism is the doctrine that experience (rather than reason, divine revelation, or any other source) is the basis of all knowledge of matters of fact (as distinct from knowledge of logical relations). The logical positivists used the new idea of logical analysis to reformulate the classical empiricism of Hume, following the lead of Russell and what they understood Ludwig Wittgenstein (1889–1951) to have meant by the aphorismic pronouncements in his *Tractatus Logico-Philosophicus* (1921), which was the focus of many Circle discussions (Hanfling, 1981).

For Hume, knowledge consisted of terms which are meaningful only when they correspond to ideas (or thoughts or concepts). Simple ideas are the remains of impressions (sensations and feelings), which are the immediate objects of our awareness and which are the sole source of knowledge of matters of fact. These immediate experiences are, then, the foundation of knowledge. Contrary to the claims of Descartes and the rationalists, we have no innate ideas. All ideas are derived from impressions. Simple ideas are their copies, and complex ideas are created by mind out of simple ideas, and thus, out of experience.

This radical empiricism was extended to modern science by natural scientists turned philosophers (Passmore, 1957, ch. 14) who were critical of the use in scientific theories of conceptions such as 'atom' or 'absolute space', for these, being beyond what is given in experience, might mislead scientists into metaphysical speculation. In Austria and Germany this form of positivism, critical not only of metaphysics but also of parts of contemporary science, became known as empiriocriticism. A typical proponent was Ernst Mach (1838–1916), who had been the first incumbent of the chair that Schlick later occupied. (Many members of the Vienna Circle were also members of the Ernst Mach Society founded with Schlick as chairman in 1928: Kraft, 1953.) Two contributions of Mach's particularly influenced the Vienna Circle. First, following Hume, he maintained that the experiences that are the foundation of science are experiences of elements of scientists' own sensations, such as colours, sounds and flavours, and not of purported real objects inaccessibly beyond experience. Experiences of sensations do not justify the suggestion that lying behind them is something, some real object, that they reflect or represent or which causes them. Such thoughts, that external objects are responsible for perceptual experiences, are complex ideas, secondary to and constructed from sensory elements. Complexes of sensory elements may be grouped together and referred to as, say, mental objects or physical objects, but this is mere convenience. There are no natural divisions between sciences, for they all study the same subject matter – the relations between sensations. This radical empiricist or phenomenalist theory of knowledge thus provides a basis for the unification of the sciences. Secondly, Mach insisted that scientists restrict themselves to attempting to achieve the most complete, precise and economical descriptions of their diverse experiences, collecting them into simple formulae. In his book *The Analysis of Sensations* (1886) he attempted to analyse the theories of mechanics, thermodynamics and optics as no more than concise statements of the covariation of sensations. His attempt stumbled, however, on the difficulty of construing the mathematical parts of the theories in these terms.

The examples of logicistic analyses of mathematics that were available to the logical positivists provided a way of overcoming Mach's difficulties, for mathematical propositions, now thought of as analytic truths, could be admitted to empirical science without tainting it metaphysically. Moreover, the Vienna Circle's members took the French mathematician Henri Poincaré (1854–1912) to suggest that the theoretical terms of science are no more than conventional tokens, exhaustively definable in terms of sensations. Consequently they believed that scientific theory, like mathematics, might be reconstructed as an axiomatic system articulated in a formal language of logic, within which correct reasoning would be precise and clear. Unlike mathematics, however, what is required in the case of scientific theory is that the ideal language of the reconstructed theory be informative, that is, say something about the experienced world. To achieve this, it is necessary to show that its primitives can be interpreted empirically. Phenomenalism seemed to provide a way of doing this. If the complex propositions in which scientific theory is expressed could be analysed into (or conversely constructed out of) sets of atomic propositions that describe immediate experience, then the ideal language would be connected to the world precisely as defined by its logical connectives. Moreover, empiricism would be vindicated: all science, that is, all systematic knowledge of non-tautological truths, would be reducible to, or constructible out of, propositions about experience. It is this task that Carnap undertook in his *The Logical Structure of the World* (1928), where he attempted to do for empirical knowledge what Whitehead and Russell had tried to do for mathematics.

The combination of phenomenalism and logicistic method is captured by the principle of verifiability, according to which the meaning of a proposition consists in how it is verified, that is, in whatever experiences show that it is true. This principle is so often taken to be the defining characteristic of logical positivism that it provides another conception of positivism, positivism$_7$. It gave the logical positivists a precise specification of positivism's anti-metaphysical programme (Carnap, 1932a). They deployed the principle as a criterion for demarcating scientific language from metaphysical and theological chatter. If a non-tautological proposition cannot in principle be verified by experience, either because it is a compound proposition employing relations that cannot be formulated in terms of ideal language connectives (that is, the proposition has an unanalysable form) or because it employs concepts that cannot be formulated in the language of experience (that is, the proposition has an unanalysable content), then it is devoid of descriptive meaning. Theological and metaphysical pseudo-propositions, being unverifiable, are neither true nor false. They are meaningless, and arguments for and against them are undecidable and therefore pointless. They might be used to express emotional attitudes, in poetry or in church, or have some other non-descriptive function, but they cannot be part of science. Metaphysics is not at fault for being emotive, for that is one of its functions. But it is at fault when it pretends to be cognitively significant. Propositions thus divide into those of logic and those of science, and all else is non-sense.

In sum, Vienna Circle positivism, like its nineteenth-century predecessor, was scientistic, naturalistic and empiricist. But, by incorporating the new logic, it became logicistic where nineteenth-century positivism had been reformist. Logic, and philosophy with it, was no longer concerned with substantive judgements, such as decisions about what social arrangements are desirable. Just as logic had been separated from the empirical study of reasoning (the science of psychology), positivist philosophy became separated from social philosophy, from comprehensive visions of how society ought to be. As Schlick (1918) stressed, philosophy was to concern itself solely with clarifying the logic of scientific inquiry. Forms of inquiry that were not scientific, such as morality and traditional metaphysics, slipped from sight, as did parts of science that were not amenable to analysis within the framework of the new logics, such as the question of scientific discovery. Philosophy of science became dominated by such issues as constructing a formal language in which all the special sciences could be unified, and relating this formal language to the world or to the language in which our experiences of the world are cast.

Logical positivism differed from the earliest Comtean forms of positivism in another respect too: it was reductionist rather than sociologistic. This came about because the logical positivists did not restrict themselves to attempting to provide a unifying *formal* language for the sciences. They also sought to establish a substantive unity. Just as the syntax of all sciences was to be the same, so too was their lexicon. All the primitives of the unifying formal language were to be interpreted, that is, given empirical meaning, in the same way. They were to be based on experiences captured in one single descriptive language. This ideal arose from Neurath's (1931a) observation that scientific propositions cannot be directly compared with experience, but only with other propositions describing those experiences. It is not sensations themselves that form the basis of science, but what the Vienna Circle called elementary or protocol sentences, sentences that are the immediate records of experience, such as 'At 3 p.m. Otto was seeing red'. The question then arose: in what vocabulary are these protocol sentences recording the foundational experiences of science to be expressed? The members of the Vienna Circle proposed different answers to this question at different times (see Chapter 5) but the important point here is that they all agreed that the different sciences should employ the same basic lexicon. Thus all the sciences should be reduced to one not only formally, but also substantively: the non-logical primitive concepts of all sciences must be interpreted in the same observational vocabulary. The outcome is that statements describing social facts, for example, are no different from statements describing psychological or any other facts. This idea of unifying the sciences both syntactically and semantically constitutes an eighth conception of positivism, though it is a conception that varies depending on the choice of formal language and the choice of descriptive vocabulary.

The logical positivists were not alone in revitalising empiricism and systematically analysing scientific knowledge in the early twentieth century. There was a parallel group in Berlin, the Association for Empirical (later Scientific) Philosophy, which met from 1928 to 1933 (Joergensen, 1951). It was organised by Hans Reichenbach (1891–1953), a great friend of Carnap's, and its most prominent members included Carl Hempel (1905–), Kurt Lewin (1890–1947) and Richard von Mises (1883–1953). They devoted themselves to detailed analyses of particular scientific concepts and theories, being more hesitant than the Vienna Circle to issue general prescriptions and prohibitions (Reichenbach, 1936).

The ideas of the Vienna Circle and Berlin Association were promulgated during the 1930s through a series of influential publications and international congresses (Joergensen, 1951; Kraft, 1953) and through visits abroad by their members and attendances at their meetings by prominent philosophers from many countries (Ayer, 1959; Feigl, 1969b). As both groups broke up under Nazi threat in the mid-1930s and their members migrated to other European countries and the USA, the logical positivist philosophy of science became established as the 'received view' (Putnam, 1962) of the natural sciences, particularly in Britain and America. A. J. Ayer (1910–), who had attended the Circle in Vienna, introduced an uncompromising phenomenalistic logical positivism to British audiences in his *Language, Truth and Logic* (1936). Although this book caused a stir at the time, probably against the background of the recent British flirtation with idealism, in general the philosophical environment in Britain, with its long tradition of empiricism, proved congenial to logical positivist ideas. In the USA a favourable reception for logical positivism had been prepared by the independent development of philosophical pragmatism, founded by Charles Sanders Peirce (1839–1914), and its descendant, the operationalism of the physicist Percy Bridgman (1882–1962). Charles Morris (1901–), who visited the Circle in Vienna, was instrumental in introducing its members to this tradition, and he himself sought to establish a position which he called scientific empiricism on the common ground between pragmatism and logical positivism (Morris, 1937). Both pragmatism and operationalism employed criteria of empirical significance that were similar to the principle of verifiability, except that they applied to concepts rather than to propositions. Peirce (1878) maintained that the meaning of a concept is given by its practical effects. Bridgman (1927) argued that we mean by a concept a set of operations, his famous example being that we mean by length the operations by which length is measured. Operationalism, in particular, found favour among American psychologists, such as E. C. Tolman (1886–1959), C. L. Hull (1884–1952) and B. F. Skinner (1904–), and some sociologists, notably G. A. Lundberg (1895–1965). All these people forged links with the emigrant members of the Vienna Circle and Berlin Association (Feigl, 1969b). But in general they derived their support for naturalism, empiricism and scientism not from the set of abstract methodological considerations that exercised the logical positivist philosophers, but from their belief that scientific inquiry would be successful, practically, if it were based on objective, value-free measurements and quantification.

LOGICAL POSITIVIST SOCIOLOGY

One of the original Vienna Circle members, Otto Neurath, paid considerable attention to the question of how sociology might be made to conform to the principles of logical positivism, in particular to his preferred physicalist variant, in which the experiences that are foundational for unified science are described in the spatio-temporal language of physics as publicly observable physical objects (Neurath, 1931a, 1931b, 1944). Sociology, like all other sciences, according to Neurath, aims to establish regularities between spatio-temporal observables, the ultimate aim of unified science being to connect together all logically compatible laws. Such a unified science, Neurath hoped, might be of practical utility in promoting progress.

Writing in the 1920s and 1930s in Vienna, where sociology and Marxism were co-extensive (Torrance, 1976), Neurath credited Marxism as being the most complete attempt to create a 'strictly scientific non-metaphysical sociology', quoting from Marx's *German Ideology* to support his claim (Neurath, 1931b, pp. 349–51). Marx's materialism, he argued, prefigures physicalism, though it has the disadvantage that it can mislead one into speculation about matter existing beyond what is experienced in the mind. Nevertheless, Neurath thought Marx's materialism preferable to the idealist counter-current represented by *verstehende* sociologists of the *Geisteswissenschaften* tradition, such as Wilhelm Dilthey (1833–1911) and Max Weber. Their anti-naturalist approach, with its insistence that human phenomena be described and understood through *verstehen*, Neurath dismissed as metaphysical.

Physicalism avoids the residual metaphysical overtones of materialism: 'mind' is not a product of 'matter'; rather, both mind and matter exist for science only in so far as they are publicly available space-time formations describable in the language of physics. Otherwise they are meaningless metaphysical concepts. The consequence is that sociology is the study of behaviour; it is social behaviourism of 'behaviouristics' as Neurath called it. All references to apparently mental events must be banished as metaphysical unless they can be replaced by behaviours describable spatio-temporally, such as speech, facial expressions and gestures, or by their physical outcomes, such as painting, books and buildings. Indeed, Neurath drew up a list of terms to be avoided because of their metaphysical flavour. He called it his *index verborum prohibitorum* and it included such words as 'mind', 'mental' and 'motive' (Hempel, 1969). These prohibitions would be relaxed, Neurath argued, only if evidence of mental states and mental events available through introspection were rendered in the language of behaviour (Feigl, 1969a; C. Taylor, 1964).

Neurath's plans for a sociology formulated in a unitary physicalist language remained programmatic, and his writings had little direct impact among early twentieth-century sociologists. Nevertheless the spirit of the age (Neurath would want that concept defined in terms of observables such as 'verbal combinations, forms of worship, modes of architecture, fashions, styles of paint-ings, etc.': Neurath, 1931a, p. 299) remained one in which those inhabiting 'backward' disciplines believed that to enjoy the success and prestige of the natural sciences they had only to articulate their problems in precise mathe-matical terms and organise their inquiries along strictly empiricist lines (C. C. Taylor, 1920). The effect of this spirit on early American sociology has been described in previous chapters. As logical positivism came to dominate the philosophy of science in the middle of the twentieth century, it undoubtedly provided reinforcement, albeit indirectly, for the notion that positivist sociology, the natural science of society, consists of the application of multivariate and inductive statistics to descriptive social statistics collected by sample surveys.

A key figure in consolidating this conception of soci-ology was Paul Lazarsfeld (1901–76), who trained as a mathematician in Vienna in the 1920s and 1930s. Although he had virtually no direct contact with the Vienna Circle, he described himself as a European positivist and recorded that he was influenced by Mach (Lazarsfeld, 1969), and he was undoubtedly influenced by the same Austro-Marxist sociology as Neurath. His energies were devoted to estab-lishing research institutes, first in Vienna, then in various centres in the USA, and finally in 1937 the Bureau of Applied Social Research at Columbia University, where he was appointed to the specially created Quételet Professor-ship in Social Sciences in 1962. His institutes mixed com-mercial market research with more academic studies funded by private foundations and by the state. By train-ing many students and producing numerous empirical research reports, the institutes played an important part in strengthening the professional identity of American sociologists around the collection and analysis of social survey data.

Lazarsfeld introduced a number of innovatory research methods. His interest was less in descriptive studies than in explanatory ones, where causal relationships between variables are identified. This led him to use multivariate analytic techniques in secondary analyses of the public opinion polls that had been growing in popularity since the 1930s, in order to separate the independent causal effects of each variable. He was particularly sensitive to the possibility of spurious or cosymptomatic relationships, where two variables covary not because one causes the other but because both are caused by a third variable, and masking, where two causally related variables are not observed to covary because of the countervailing effects of a third variable. To guard against these possibilities, Lazarsfeld recommended a stepwise analytic procedure, where one starts with a relation between two variables and then partitions it by the introduction of a third variable in an attempt to interpret or explain away the original relationship (Lazarsfeld, 1955).

In his research into people's voting intentions and into the effects of radio broadcasts, Lazarsfeld introduced the use of panel methods, in which the same people are interviewed on several successive occasions. He thought of these as natural field experiments (analogous to the agricultural experiments which had prompted earlier developments in statistics). By explicitly introducing time as a variable, panel methods enabled causes to be distinguished from their subsequent effects (Lazarsfeld, 1948). Alongside panels, he also used control groups, who were interviewed less often than the panel, so allowing changes that resulted from interviewing itself, rather than from other causes, to be isolated. All these tools became part of the standard repertoire of the professional sociologist, and prepared the way for further developments in the application of statistical methods to social data, such as causal modelling.

In sum: within sociology, positivism remained the description of a set of practical techniques for the collection and manipulation of social data, in particular the use of sample surveys to generate descriptive social statistics which are then analysed using multivariate and inductive statistics to induce generalisations or test hypotheses (positivism$_6$). With the logical positivists, however, positivism came to be a programme for demarcating science from metaphysics by deploying the principle of verifiability (positivism$_7$) and unifying the special sciences around a common syntax, for example, the *Principia* logic, and a common vocabulary, for example, that of the physicalist language (positivism$_8$). Working out the details of this programme came to dominate the philosophy of science by the mid-twentieth century, and it is to some of these details that I turn in the next two chapters.

4

Laws and Explanation

For many authors, the term positivism has been associated with the idea that laws have a central place in science. 'Positivism' has been understood to apply only to inquiries into issues that can be decided by appeal to experience, and the honorific title 'science' has been reserved for descriptions of what is experienced, expressed in concise and precise formulae or laws. Paradigmatic for Comte, for example, were Newton's laws of motion, for Comte probably accepted Newton's claim that he derived these laws inductively from experience, a claim that Newton deliberately opposed to Descartes' suggestion that the basic laws of physics are deductively derived from indubitable metaphysical principles.

Mach, however, criticised Newton's laws from a thoroughgoing phenomenalist point of view. Newton had maintained that his laws of motion specified how bodies move in absolute space and absolute time, two notions that Mach rejected because of their metaphysical flavour. He sought to reconstruct mechanics as a set of purely empirical generalisations in which absolute space was replaced by spatial intervals measured relative to 'fixed' stars and absolute time replaced by temporal intervals measured by physical processes (Mach, 1883). For Mach, scientific laws must be no more than summary descriptions, comprehensive and condensed reports of experience. The logical positivists agreed. For Carnap, for example, laws are simply descriptions of observed regularities (Carnap, 1966).

Knowledge of laws is taken to be the aim of positive science because laws provide the basis of explanations and also enable us to anticipate phenomena, that is, predict their occurrence and thereby ultimately control them. The first detailed formal analysis of the role of laws in explanation and prediction, by Carl Hempel (1905–), came in the 1940s in the wake of logical positivism, though the main points of the analysis had already been outlined by Karl Popper (1902–) in his *The Logic of Scientific Discovery*, published in Vienna in 1934, and had appeared informally in the writings of earlier positivists back to Comte.

In his celebrated analysis, Hempel (1942; Hempel and Oppenheim, 1948) proposed that sound explanations must fulfil four conditions. Three are logical conditions: first, the explanans must entail the explanandum; second, the explanans must contain general laws which are necessary for the deduction of the explanandum (in the case of the explanation of singular phenomenon rather than of laws, the explanans also contains non-law statements describing antecedent conditions); and third, the explanans must be capable of empirical test. The fourth, empirical condition is that the explanans must be true. These conditions, argues Hempel, apply equally to prediction, the only difference being the time at which the explanans is given relative to the occurrence of the phenomenon described in the explanandum. If the explanans comes first, then one has a prediction, but if the explanandum phenomenon occurs first, then one has an explanation.

There are several desiderata for laws which facilitate explanation and prediction in the Hempelian sense, although unlike the truth requirement they are not necessary features (Achinstein, 1971). They are that laws should be simple, specifying simple relations between a limited number of factors; they should be precise, preferably specifying mathematically the relation between quantitatively measured observations; they should be economical, that is, general in scope in the sense of summarising and relating the least restricted range of observations; and they should be universal, that is, they should apply to all the phenomena within their range without exception. (A law can have a restricted scope but be universal. The most general laws are unrestricted and universal.)

According to Hempel his four conditions, which he summarises in the deductive-nomological (D-N) schema portrayed in Figure 4.1, capture the essential features of explanation and prediction that are common to all the sciences. The schema, therefore, provides a basis for the unification of the sciences, and it also embodies a ninth conception of positivism: positivism$_9$ is a theory of knowledge according to which science consists of a corpus of interrelated, true, simple, precise and wide-ranging universal laws that are central to explanation and prediction in the manner described in the D-N schema.

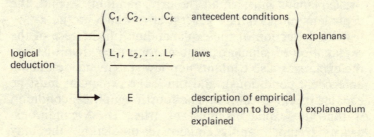

Figure 4.1   *The deductive-nomological schema.*

The claim that the sciences can be unified around the D-N schema has been accepted by some sociologists, most notably by George Homans (1910–), who emphasises that sociology is not radically different from natural sciences because, like all sciences, it seeks to construct D-N explanations (Homans, 1964, 1967). Homans also offers an extended analysis of a number of empirical sociological research studies in an attempt to show that their findings can be explained by five general laws of human behaviour, in the sense of being deduced from them under the appropriate initial conditions. Homans's laws are taken from behavioural psychology and utilitarian economics (Homans, 1961). But independent of the recommendations and analyses of this one sociologist, the D-N schema has

become well known to sociologists for another reason –
because it features in several philosophy of social science
textbooks as their characterisation of science (Rudner,
1966; Lessnoff, 1974; Studdert-Kennedy, 1975). Moreover,
the D-N schema is likely to be viewed sympathetically by
those sociologists who are persuaded that the aim of
scientific research is to establish empirical generalisations
or laws in order to explain and predict (Wallace, 1971), this
being a formulation favoured by authors of social research
methods texts (see, as two examples out of many, Smith,
1975; Black and Champion, 1976). Yet despite the advice
in these texts on how to organise research to generate and
test regularities, and despite the lists of putative laws
provided by Popper (1944–5, pp. 62–3), Williams (1947),
Joynt and Rescher (1959, pp. 386–7) and Berelson and
Steiner (1964), the paucity of sociological laws that com-
bine the virtues of empirical truth, simplicity, generality,
precision and universality is well known. Indeed, these
features seem to be alternatives in sociology: some can be
secured only if others are relinquished (Lessnoff, 1974).
For example, Homans's law, his 'success proposition'
according to which 'for all actions taken by persons, the
more often a particular action of a person is rewarded, the
more likely the person is to perform that action' (Homans,
1961, p. 16) is simple (two variables: rewards and performance of action) and general (for *all* actions), but it fails to
fulfil the desiderata of universality (the result is only 'more
likely') and precision (neither rewards nor the relation
between them and performance is specified), and it
possibly violates the requirement of empirical truth. On
the other hand, the laws resulting from causal modelling
(see below) are often precise, sometimes universal, but
rarely simple or general, and whether or not they are
empirically true depends upon the various assumptions
that have to be made to complete the statistical analysis.
Given these shortcomings, it is appropriate to inquire
further into the nature of laws and their role in explanation.

More is required of laws than that they possess the
virtues listed earlier. The explanatory force and predictive

capacity of the D-N schema relies on laws holding with some sort of necessity that licenses inferences from antecedent to consequent: given the antecedent, the consequent *must* occur. In the absence of this necessity one is left with mere accidental generalisations, where the occurrence of the antecedent gives no guarantee that the consequent will follow, so that even if the consequent does occur, it cannot be said to have occurred because of the antecedent. Characterising the required form of necessity, has, however, proved difficult.

The difficulty was particularly severe for the logical positivists because they attempted to formalise scientific laws using the *Principia* logic. Consequently, they were limited to specifying the relationship embodied in laws as material implication, which is symbolised $\supset$ or $\Rightarrow$ and defined as in Table 4.1. Material implication, meaning no

Table 4.1   *Definition of the Logical Relation of Material Implication*

If proposition p is	and proposition q is	then proposition $p \supset q$ is
true	true	true
true	false	false
false	true	true
false	false	true

more than the exclusion of the joint truth of p and falsity of q, is a very weak relation, weaker even than the verbal expression it is often taken to represent, namely, 'if p, then q'. As a result, although material implication proved useful in the analysis of mathematics, by taking '$p \supset q$' as a model of the simplest type of scientific law, logical positivists found it impossible to distinguish formally between laws and accidental generalisations. Despite this, there is heavy reliance upon material implication in the few sociological writings where formalisation is attempted (Stinchcombe, 1968; Abell, 1971), perhaps because of the positivists' ideal of mathematicising sociological theories, in accordance with the desideratum that laws be precise (Zetterberg, 1954; Blalock, 1969).

Is there some criterion that can be added to distinguish laws from accidental generalisations? One approach to this question is to argue that if regularities are to be laws they must support counterfactual conditionals, and accidental generalisations do not do this (Kneale, 1950). Only if 'all A are B' is a law does it entail that 'if C, which is not an A, were an A, then it would be a B'. But there is a problem with this approach which is that it relies upon an independent understanding of counterfactuals. Some interpretations of them are plainly inadequate. For example, since hypothetical universals expressed as material implications are trivially or vacuously true if the antecedent is false (see the bottom two lines of Table 4.1), it follows that if counterfactual conditionals are interpreted as the conjunction of a material conditional and a denial of the antecedent, then any generalisation would entail counterfactuals. That is, entailment of counterfactuals interpreted this way would not discriminate between laws and non-laws. The question then is whether there is some alternative interpretation of counterfactuals which re-establishes their discriminatory power. Although some such alternatives have been offered (Mackie, 1974), it appears that the decision whether or not a particular generalisation does support a particular counterfactual is based ultimately on a prior decision as to the lawfulness of the universal under consideration. In other words, it is doubtful whether there is an analysis of counterfactuals independent of lawfulness which would allow their use as a test of lawfulness.

Another way of attempting to identify the necessity that characterises laws but is absent from accidental generalisations is in terms of causality, even though there might be laws that are non-causal – for example, laws of coexistence, laws of functional relationship and Comte's relations of similarity – and some singular causal statements might not be instances of causal regularities, even implicitly. Nevertheless, the idea of causality is so commonly linked with positivism that another conception of positivism, the tenth, is that it is a theory of knowledge according to which science consists of a corpus of causal laws on the basis of which phenomena are explained and predicted. Yet many early positivists were antithetical to causality because of its mysterious, metaphysical undertones. Comte, for example, insisted that making laws the goal of science involves abandoning the search for causes, which are inaccessible and meaningless (Comte, 1830). Russell (1917) held that causal talk belongs to pre-scientific discourse, and 'causality' featured on Neurath's *index verborum prohibitorum*.

These hesitations undoubtedly spring from the empiricist analysis of causation, initially articulated by Hume, who found the idea (concept) of causal relation to be a complex one, compounded of three simple ideas: temporal priority, contiguity and necessary connection. The first two of these simple ideas are straightforwardly based on impressions (that is, experiences) of time sequences between events and their relative spatial locations. Hume maintained that the last, however, is not derived from experience, for necessity is not observable. When watching billiard balls bumping into each other, we experience changes in the spatio-temporal relations between the balls, but we do not observe necessary connections. The most that we can experience is the repetition of instances of the co-occurrence of the same types of event – constant conjunctions of events – but there are no impressions from which the idea of necessary connection could be derived. We see no intimate tie, no continuous connecting process or cement joining one event (a cause) to another event (its effect). Where, then, does our idea of necessary connection come from? Hume insists that it cannot be a logical relation (an analytic *a priori* relation), because the occurrence of an event described independently of other events entails neither the occurrence nor the non-occurrence of any other events. Hume's view is that the observation of the constant conjunction of two types of event gives rise to a mental habit or psychological propensity of expecting this regularity to be repeated. The necessity is, then, a feature of the human mind, which is unwittingly transferred into the real world of events. Although our *idea* of causation includes the notion of necessity, causal connection in the world, according to Hume, is no more than constant conjunction of contiguous and consecutive, but logically and materially independent, events. The necessity that appears to be a property of regularities of succession is not located in the empirical world, but is a psychological addition by the observer.

Hume's inquiry into the notion of causation can be recast in terms of a logical positivist analysis of the language of science (Radnitzky, 1968). Hume, with whom Mill agreed but Comte, Russell and Neurath disagreed, begins by admitting that scientific knowledge includes causal sentences and he offers an empiricist analysis of causal terms. He denies that causal terms are logical connectives, part of the formal language of science. If causal terms are non-logical and if they are not to be metaphysical nonsense, then they must be part of the descriptive vocabulary of science. Cause is not, however, a primitive descriptive term, for it does not refer to something of which we have direct awareness. Cause is a non-primitive term, defined by Hume as the conjunction of three primitives: temporal sequence, spatial proximity and repeated co-occurrence of types of event. The term 'cause' is, then, strictly redundant, as it can be eliminated from scientific sentences by explicit definition in terms of these three primitives. This was the logical positivists' initial but ultimately unsuccessful approach to all theoretical terms in science (see Chapter 5) and it is arguable that the various criticisms of Hume's analysis of causality (to be explored below) are but instances of the general failings of this eliminative approach to theory.

Logical positivists adopted this Humean analysis when they restricted the formal language of science to the extensional logic of the *Principia* and represented laws as material implication sentences. Cause, being a modal term, cannot be captured in extensional logic, and had therefore to be a descriptive term if it were to be meaningful. Some twentieth-century positivists adopted an alternative approach, however. By supplementing the *Principia* logic with modal operators, they were able to take cause to be a logical, not a descriptive term (Reichenbach, 1954). Whether the new systems of logic, embracing causal implication, are free from paradoxes remains contentious, though some authors believe that it is in further developments of non-extensional modal logic that a successful analysis of causality will be found (Burks, 1977).

Hume's psychological presuppositions about the relations between impressions and ideas have been criticised, but it is now generally accepted that these are not essential to his central thesis that causal regularities or laws can be explicated without recourse to irreducible modal notions like natural necessity (Mackie, 1974). Nevertheless, the issue remains as to whether the three features of temporal sequence, contiguity and constant conjunction are the identifying characteristics of causal regularities that distinguish them from non-causal ones.

It is nowadays usually conceded (though there is still dispute on the issue) that Hume's arguments for causes preceding their effects, and for distant causes being linked to their effects by an intervening chain of proximate causes, are invalid: causes can act at a distance, both spatially and temporally, and causes and effects can overlap temporally, even to the extent of occurring simultaneously. (Whether effects can precede their causes is more controversial.) All that remains of the Humean view of cause, then, is that causal regularities are to be distinguished solely by virtue of being constant conjunctions of types of event. Whether or not this is the case is difficult to establish, not least because of imprecisions in Hume's own account (Mackie, 1974, ch. 1). In particular, it is unclear whether, in maintaining that two types of event are constantly conjoined, Hume was claiming that events of one type are necessary, or sufficient, or necessary and sufficient for the occurrence of events of the other type, where condition C is necessary for E if, invariably, whenever E occurs, C occurs, and condition C is sufficient for E if, invariably, whenever C occurs, E occurs. (Necessity is used here to describe a type of condition – event, state, phenomenon, or process – for the occurrence of some other type of event, which is a different sense of necessity from earlier, when it was used to describe the difference between a law and a non-law. Talk of events being necessary or sufficient conditions for the occurrence of other events is not without problems, particularly about ontological presuppositions: see Kim, 1971.)

Yet unfortunately for the Humean account, it would appear that none of the three resulting accounts of constant conjunction succeeds in separating causal from non-causal regularities. If a cause is a type of event that is both necessary and sufficient for the type of event that is its effect, then our idea that the relation between cause and effect is asymmetrical (C being the cause of the effect E does not entail that E is the cause of C) is lost, for necessary and sufficient condition is a symmetrical relation (if C is necessary and sufficient for E, then E is sufficient and necessary for C, because necessary and sufficient conditions are the reverse of each other). To retain the asymmetry of causal regularities, necessary and sufficient conditionship must be supplemented by some additional feature, such as Hume's idea of sequentiality. But if it is granted that cause and effect can be entirely contemporaneous, that is, if sequentiality as a characteristic of causal regularities is abandoned, then causal priority has to be formulated in some other way, compatible with the simultaneous occurrence of cause and effect. It is doubtful whether this can be done without invoking some intrinsic or natural necessity in causal relations between events in the world, that steps outside the Humean framework.

The task of locating an additional asymmetric feature of causality, beyond necessary and sufficient conditionship, can be avoided by taking constant conjunction to mean necessary condition, which is an asymmetrical relation. But another problem then obtrudes: that of overdetermination. Conditions that, when they occur separately, are necessary for E (that is, cause E) are no longer necessary for E (that is, do not cause E) if they occur simultaneously. The usual example is of two bullets entering a person's heart simultaneously: either bullet arriving separately would have been the cause of (a necessary condition for) death, but when both penetrate together neither is necessary (is the cause) because the arrival of the other would have resulted in death (Scriven, 1966).

Sufficient condition, too, is asymmetrical, but suffers the problem of allowing the inclusion among constant conjunctions of undeterminative (or non-causal) regularities: in many cases where the condition C is sufficient for E (that is, causes E), E is also sufficient for C, even though we would not want to say that E causes C. For example, the motion of a car to which is hitched a caravan is sufficient for the motion of the caravan. But also, given that they are hitched together, the motion of the caravan is sufficient for the motion of the car. Nevertheless, while we would be prepared to say that the car's moving (pulling) caused the caravan to move, we would be reluctant to say that the caravan's moving (being pulled) caused the car to move. In other words, some additional feature is required to distinguish the causal connection from the non-causal one (R. Taylor, 1966).

Characterising cause in terms of necessary condition includes too much: when inquiring why a house caught fire, a necessary condition is that oxygen was present, as is that the house existed, but while these might be included among the causal factors, or initial conditions, for the fire, it would not always be appropriate to identify either of them as *the* cause. Also, a set of necessary conditions might have to co-occur before they are, jointly, sufficient for their effect. It is complications such as these that Mill (1843, bk III) took account of in his analysis of cause. As Mill recognised, an effect might be connected with an 'assemblage of conditions' (a conjunction of causes) or with 'a plurality of causes' (different independent causes) and it might occur only if certain 'countervailing causes' are absent. These complications are brought together in constant conjunctions of the form 'all $AB\bar{C}$ or $DF\bar{G}$ or $HI\bar{J}$

are followed by E', where $\overline{C}$ symbolises not-C or the absence of an event of type C and where each antecedent (A, B, etc.) is an 'inus' condition for E, that is, an insufficient but non-redundant part of a joint condition (for example, $AB\overline{C}$) which is itself unnecessary but sufficient for the result E (Mackie, 1965). An example might be provided by a theory of revolution that combines ideas from Marxism and from relative deprivation theory and argues that revolutionary activity (E) follows *either* the joint occurrence of the polarisation of capitalist society into two classes, the bourgeoisie and the proletariat (A), the immiseration of the proletariat (B) and the absence of proletarian false consciousness ($\overline{C}$) *or* the joint occurrence of the division of society into a hierarchy of groups (D), conformity of members of one group to the norms of another, higher group (F) and the absence of routes of mobility from the lower to the higher group ($\overline{G}$). Other theories of revolution, which might be thought to be in competition with the two components of this combined theory, can be added as extra sets of inus conditions (for example, $HI\overline{J}$).

The advantage of incorporating the complications that Mill highlights into the conception of constant conjunction is that the task of specifying inus conditions better represents the scientist's search for causes. Empirical inquiry often results in the claim that A causes E, not in the sense of being a necessary and/or sufficient condition for E, but in the sense that A is an inus condition for E, without it being possible to specify what other non-redundant factors occurring jointly with A are necessary for E and without being able to exclude the possibility that there are other sets of conditions (for example, $DF\overline{G}$) whose occurrence is minimally sufficient for E. In other words, empirical inquiry is often devoted to filling out elliptical laws like 'all A . . . $\overline{B}$ . . . or D . . . $\overline{G}$ or . . . are followed by E', by utilising Mill's methods, for example (see Chapter 5).

Nevertheless, constant conjunctions of even this complicated sort suffer the same problems faced by those of simpler kinds: they all fail to separate causal laws from accidental generalisations. There are still regularities, including regularities of succession that incorporate the asymmetry normally thought of as a characteristic of causality, that are not causal laws but accidental generalisations and spurious correlations. Common examples are day following night, and green traffic lights following red ones.

In sum, the Humean analysis of causation in terms of constant conjunction fails to distinguish laws from accidental regularities. Faced with this conclusion, four courses are available, two Humean and two non-Humean. One course is to maintain that there is no distinction, a heroic Humean stand (Mackie, 1974) that amounts to asserting that everything happens in accordance with causal laws so that any regularity whatsoever expresses a lawful connection. In other words, the most accidental appearing of universals are laws. But even Humeans mostly prefer to adopt an alternative course, that involves searching for some additional logical or epistemic criterion that differentiates regularities that are laws from those that are accidental generalisations.

In terms of logical requirements, attempts have been made to specify an intrinsic grammatical form for laws, for example, unrestricted universality, but no such syntactical criterion has yet been identified that successfully demarcates between laws and accidental generalisations. Alternatively, it has been suggested that laws, but not accidental generalisations, can be derived from higher-level laws, that is, they fit into a deductive system of laws. However, as a logical requirement, this fails because an accidental generalisation is deducible from premises that contain higher-level accidental generalisations. The only way of applying this distinguishing criterion is, then, to argue that there are some fundamental laws, at the highest possible level, that are indubitably laws and that these supply the premises that ensure the lawfulness of all generalisations deduced from them. This is the approach that Mill adopted to solve the problem of induction (see Chapter 5) but it is circular in so far as it relies upon an unexplicated notion of lawfulness at the highest level through which to explicate lawfulness at deductively lower levels.

Given the persistent failure of attempts to locate intrinsic formal characteristics that separate laws from accidental generalisations (Nagel, 1961), some Humeans have searched instead for epistemic or contextual criteria of lawfulness. It is argued, for example, that attributions of lawfulness come from the place of statements within a specific context of scientific knowledge (Braithwaite, 1953, ch. 9): a law is a universal statement that integrates with, by being deducible from, a coherent set of laws that constitutes an accepted body of scientific knowledge. On this view, a universal is a law when it is doubly empirically certified: both directly and also indirectly by the empirical evidence for the other generalisations within the accepted body of knowledge. Unfortunately, however, this demarcation criterion, and modifications of it, also seem to fail in so far as it is possible to construct counter-examples, that is, cases that are intuitively non-lawful but which fulfil this requirement of indirect evidential support from the context of scientific knowledge (Harré and Madden, 1975).

Given the continuing arguments that Humeans fail to find either intrinsic formal or epistemic criteria that unambiguously identify which statements of constant conjunction are laws and which merely accidental generalisations, one of the alternative, non-Humean courses is to insist that 'cause' is a primitive idea that is intelligible without analysis. In other words, Hume's analysis, it is argued, is otiose, for cause is not a notion that must be founded in experience or rejected as meaningless metaphysics. Instead, being independently understandable, causality can serve as a criterion of lawfulness (Anscombe, 1971). One might arrive at this view after attempting to analyse causality in terms of counterfactual implication or of production, since these notions simply return to one of the primitive idea of cause (R. Taylor, 1966). Critics of this view simply press their empiricist (Humean) reservations and demand an analysis: what is this thing, causality, and what guide does it give, in empirical inquiry, to identifying those connections between events that are lawful and so may be used for explanation and prediction?

The second non-Humean course is to offer an analysis of causal connection that extends beyond the restrictions of the Humean framework in one of two possible directions: the rationalists suggest that the necessity that distinguishes causal laws from accidental generalisations is logical necessity, while the realists suggest that it is physical necessity.

If the necessity of laws is logical – if they are necessarily true because they are the laws of our faculty of reason, or in a more modern idiom, because they are the laws of our language use – then they are clearly separable from merely *de facto*, contingent regularities. But whereas anti-Humean rationalists argue that laws are indubitable metaphysical principles known to be true *a priori* (that is, non-inductively), positivists reject any suggestion that such statements could be synthetic or empirically significant, describing necessary connections between events in the world or between sense-data knowable without recourse to empirical investigation. Humean empiricists maintain that at the most, some apparent laws may be tautologies, analytic *a priori* statements or definitions that are empty of empirical content, being merely part of the syntactical rules of science. But for Hempelians, these cannot be described as laws, for they violate the requirement of the D-N schema which insists that they be empirically testable: laws must be synthetic *a posteriori*. The Humean objection to the idea of logical necessity seems to stand: there can be no logically necessary connection between the descriptions of intrinsically independent events. The necessity, the Humean therefore concludes, must be an extrinsic addition, supplied by the observer.

To counter this claim, anti-Humean realists argue that the necessity that divides laws from non-laws reflects the real power of causes to produce their effects (Harré, 1961). Cause and effect are not independent, but are intrinsically related. Part of what it is to be a particular cause is to have the power to bring about its particular effect, there being a real connection between cause and effect, a generative mechanism (which need not, of course, be mechanical) linking cause to its effect. On this view, regular connection and perhaps temporal succession may be evidence for a causal relation, but they do not constitute its meaning, which derives from the natural mechanism connecting the cause and effect. For the realist, the requirements of the D-N schema, although necessary for explanation, are sufficient only if the laws of nature on which explanations depend describe physically necessary connections in the real world, such that given the cause the effect will naturally occur, unless something interferes with the working of the connecting mechanism.

In sum: both the rationalist and the realist conceptions of laws solve the problems encountered in the Humean analysis, but only by stepping outside the framework of that analysis. The rationalist view that laws express logically necessary connections differs from the Humean analysis of causation in that it no longer gives epistemological priority to experience and instead affords reason the ability to contribute to the content of science. Those who subscribe to positivism$_2$ are unwilling to allow reason any role other than tracing logical relations between empirically based atoms of knowledge, for they fear that reason is a source of unreason, of bias and prejudice, when uncontrolled by experience. On the other hand, the realist view that laws describe natural necessary connections differs from the Humean analysis of causation in that it no longer gives ontological priority to observable atomic events and instead treats events as intrinsically related through underlying generative mechanisms. Those who subscribe to positivism$_2$ are unwilling to grant the existence of such imputed mechanisms and invisible powers, for they fear that they are metaphysical ghosts, too easily invoked as pseudo-explanations unless controlled by experience.

CAUSE IN SOCIOLOGY

There is some tendency among sociologists to adopt a

heroic Humean stance, for example, when they simply collect data and correlate variables, and perhaps test for statistical significance, but pay less explicit attention to substantive significance. In such cases, where no assessment is made of why some variables are correlated and others are not, there does seem to be an assumption that all (or all statistically significant) correlations are causal laws. Less heroic, but still Humean, are those who insist that only universal regularities have the correct form to be acceptable as laws. They seek to render correlation coefficients near unity by adding initial conditions and refining the measures of the variables under consideration (as described by Boudon, 1971, ch. 4). In effect, they restrict the range of their regularities and remove measurement errors in an attempt to achieve universality.

In contrast, much of the sociological literature concerned with avoiding spurious correlation (Lazarsfeld, 1955) and with inferring causality from correlation (Blalock, 1964) through *ex post facto* statistical analyses is predicated upon the assumption that social laws, if they are to feature in adequate explanations, have to express causal relations that are stronger than mere covariation, even universal covariation. Yet the conception of cause adopted often remains Humean. For example, in causal modelling or path analysis (which are, effectively, generalisations of Lazarsfeld's techniques of elaborating statistical relationships to reveal spuriousness, and so on: H. A. Simon, 1954), the existence (or strength) of regularities is identified by using multivariate statistics to obtain measures of correlation between every possible pair of variables in the set under consideration. The values of the correlation measures are then used to choose between alternative causal models, that is, between alternative sets of assumptions (or theories) about which network of causes was responsible for the data. The overall aim is to delete from the network of all possible causal connections between the variables under consideration those that do not exist (or that do not exist above a chosen limit of strength). But then the problem facing all Humeans arises:

statistical operations on observed data isolate regularities but do not distinguish between causal and non-causal conjunctions. Confronted by this problem, causal modellers typically turn to the sort of additional criteria invoked by Humeans to supplement regularity in their analyses of causality. One such criterion is causal priority interpreted as temporal order: some variables, it is argued, naturally occur prior to others and so can cause them but cannot be caused by them, this being the sociologists' equivalent of Hume's addition of sequence to constant conjunctions. For example, education measured in years of schooling comes naturally, it is said, before occupational status measured in terms of level of earnings and so, if the two are correlated, the former causes the latter but not vice versa. Alternatively, causal priority is sometimes interpreted as the theoretical order among the variables. It is argued that there is some theoretical reason, perhaps established in earlier research, for explicitly including or excluding some variables or relations between variables, this being the sociologists' equivalent of the Humean philosophers maintaining that laws must be embedded in a contextual system of accepted laws or theory. For example, on the basis of earlier empirical work, the rewards accruing to natural scientists are said to be caused only indirectly by the quality of their work, the direct cause being other scientists' perceptions of the quality of their work (J. R. Cole, 1979, p. 127).

Causal modelling is the most recent development of the sixth conception of positivism, according to which science consists of the statistical manipulation of quantified data (Mullins, 1973, ch. 9). It was extended to sociology in America primarily by two people: O. Dudley Duncan (1921–) who was trained by Ogburn in the late 1940s and who was influenced by path analysis in biology (Duncan, 1966), and Hubert M. Blalock (1926–) who originally trained in mathematics and physics and who was influenced by econometrics, especially the work of Herbert Simon (1916–). (There are differences in approach between these two authors and between them and the notable French pro-

proponent of causal modelling, Raymond Boudon, but these difficulties can be safely ignored here.) Its application to social data depended at least partly on the availability from the early 1960s onwards of computers to perform routine statistical calculations.

The procedures involved in causal modelling can be illustrated by considering the case of three measured variables, X, Y and Z, and the three unmeasured disturbance or stochastic or error variables U_1, U_2 and U_3 associated with them. U_1 summarises all the other variables, including those that cause measurement errors, that account for variations in X but which have not been explicitly identified or included in the analysis, though they could be added later. U_2 and U_3 have a similar meaning for Y and Z respectively. If one is able to assume (1) that the relations between all the variables are linear; (2) that the effects on each variable of the others are additive, that is, that each is an unnecessary but sufficient condition for the others, and that none is an insufficient but non-redundant part of a set of conditions that are jointly minimally

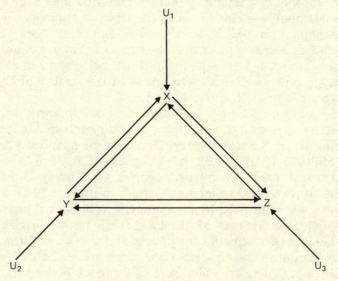

Figure 4.2 *A simple causal model.*

sufficient for the others; and (3) that no component of U_1 has an effect either on any component of U_2 or U_3, or on Y or Z except via X, and similarly for U_2 and U_3, then the set of all possible causal relations between the variables can be represented by the arrows linking them in Figure 4.2. (Causal arrows from X to U_1, Y to U_2 and X to U_3 are excluded by the first part of assumption (1). If they were included, U_2, for example, would have causal effects on U_1, via Y and X, and via Y, Z and X.) The assumptions (1) to (3) can be relaxed, at the cost of adding considerable complications which will not be examined here.

This causal network can be represented by the following set of mathematical propositions.

$$X = a_X + b_{XY.Z}Y + b_{XZ.Y}Z + u_X$$

$$Y = a_Y + b_{YX.Z}X + b_{YZ.X}Z + u_Y$$

$$Z = a_Z + b_{ZX.Y}X + b_{ZY.X}Y + u_Z$$

Attempts to solve this set of simultaneous regression equations face what is known as the identification problem: the values of u and of the coefficients a and b cannot be determined unless further simplifying assumptions are made, as there are too many 'unknowns' (too many values to calculate – in this case twelve) compared with the empirical information available, which consists of the correlation measures for each pair of the measured variables (in this case three). The identification problem can be solved only if the number of unknowns is less than or equal to the number of equations. If there are too many unknowns (under-identification) there will be infinitely many sets of possible coefficient values compatible with the empirical information, and more simplifying assumptions have to be made to avoid this possibility.

Assuming that each variable is measured in terms of standard deviation units from its mean, that is, that it is standardised, means that $a_X = a_Y = a_Z = 0$, which disposes of three unknowns. Assuming that there are no two-way causal connections and no feedback loops, that is, that the system is recursive, means that if $b_{ij.k} \neq 0$ then $b_{ji.k} = 0$, which disposes of three more unknowns. (As sociological theory develops, it might be possible to give the a and b coefficients theoretically determined non-zero values.) Assuming that the disturbance terms in all the equations do not covary, that is, that $\mathrm{cov}(u_X u_Y) = \mathrm{cov}(u_Y u_Z) = \mathrm{cov}(u_Z u_X) = 0$, which is guaranteed by assumption (3) above, disposes of a further three unknowns. The remaining three b values (called path coefficients) can then be calculated. But even though a unique set of path coefficients has now been identified, still more assumptions have to be made, for more than one causal model is compatible with this set of b values. This is because mathematical relations are symmetrical whereas causal ones are asymmetrical. To achieve the required asymmetry, one has to order the variables on the basis of assumptions about causal priority, derived perhaps from their natural temporal order or in the light of some accepted theory. Thus, even in the case where only two causal links are operative between the three measured variables, there are twelve possible causal models, and only if one can make the additional minimal assumptions that X is an independent or exogenous variable (that is, that it can cause but cannot be caused by Y and Z) and that Y is a dependent or endogenous variable (that is, that it can be caused by but cannot cause X and Z) can one limit the range of possible alternatives to the three shown in Figure 4.3. One can then select between these on the basis of the empirical information given by the correlation coefficients r_{XY}, r_{XZ} and r_{YZ}.

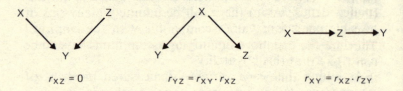

Figure 4.3 *Three causal models.*

What this case illustrates is not only the technical complexity of the Humean sociologist's task, but also that it is only after many assumptions have been made that alternative causal models can be excluded (or falsified). It might be that several of the assumptions are unrealistic in sociology. Yet in their defence, Humeans argue that simplification enhances clarity in the initial stages of inquiry. Causal modelling has the advantage of providing an exact statement, and a precise test, of theory, and there are no *a priori* reasons why the assumptions cannot be progressively relaxed as inquiry proceeds (D. A. Kenny, 1979). More complicated models can be constructed, involving non-additive and non-linear relations between more variables (for example, inus-type laws) and where the initially unmeasured disturbance variables are unpacked into measured variables so that what is left of them is responsible for only very little of the variability of the measured variables. The only ineradicable assumptions are those that face any Humean attempting to separate causal from non-causal regularities. This involves finding some logical or epistemic criterion to add, the favourite being causal priority, identified either in terms of observed temporal priority or empirically pre-established 'theoretical' priority.

Non-Humean approaches to causality are also represented in sociology. The idea that causal connections are logically necessary is adopted by those who maintain that actions are to be explained by identifying the reasons, motives, purposes, or intentions (the distinctions between which can be safely ignored here) of the actors who perform them, and that these reasons and so on are not Humean causes but intrinsic features of the actions (Peters, 1958; Melden, 1961; A. J. P. Kenny, 1963; Louch, 1966). Reasons are logically connected to actions. They are the meanings of the actions that at least in part constitute the actions as the actions they are. For example, the very possibility of performing the action of marrying relies on a set of constitutive rules that make it that action rather than another, just as the rules of cricket make playing cricket possible (Searle, 1972). Sociology is then said to consist of the explication of the constitutive rules of action that make up a culture (Winch, 1958).

Humean critics counter that while it is important to begin by identifying the meanings of actions in culturally appropriate terms, that is only a starting point and the sociologist must go on from there and search for the social or economic or material (or whatever) determinants of these meanings (Abel, 1948; Kaplan, 1964). For example, why do members of that culture marry – what causes them to perform that action? Moreover, Humeans maintain that even if under some descriptions the reason for an action is logically connected to (for example, is constitutive of) the action, there are other descriptions of either the reason or the action under which they are linked only contingently. In other words, entertaining the reason and performing the action can be distinct events and one can then investigate whether the reason is in fact the Humean cause of the action (Davidson, 1963; Ayer, 1967). For example, is the reason 'fulfilment in love' the cause of the action of attending a registry office and repeating various sentences?

In sociology, the view that causal laws describe real generative mechanisms is adopted by those who maintain that actions are to be explained by identifying the reasons of the actors who perform them, and that these reasons are not Humean causes but describe powers of agency that produce actions as their observable effects (Harré and Secord, 1972). For example, actors, given their assessment of the alternative courses of action available to them and given their preferences, have reason to marry, and this reason generates their action of marrying. Sociology is then said to consist of identifying the actors' subjective meanings, their beliefs and preferences, as these are the real causes of their actions. Weber (1914) seems to subscribe to this as one part of his conception of sociological explanation: he requires that explanations in sociology be not only causally adequate, in the Humean sense of there

being a regular connection between antecedent and consequent, but also adequate at the level of meaning, in the
sense that the observed correlation must be supplemented
by identifying the actors' mental states that generate their
actions. In the absence of an understanding of the actors'
motives, Weber insists that regularities, however general,
remain sociologically unintelligible, that is, they do not
provide sociological explanations. Humean critics counter
that the mental states of other persons are empirically
inaccessible. In taking this view, they are simply pressing
their empiricist objections to the postulation of potentially
metaphysical unobservables as the explainers of observable
phenomena like human behaviour – recall Comte's objections to the psychology of his day.

The view that causal laws describe real generative
mechanisms is adopted also by those who maintain that
actions and institutions are to be explained by identifying
the underlying social or economic or material or whatever
structures which generate them. In other words, the
powers of agency that are causally responsible for observed
actions and institutions are extended from individual
actors' reasons to the social or economic or material
structures of whole societies. Marx's work is interpreted
this way when it is suggested that what he did was to
elucidate the internal causal structures of various modes of
production, each of which generates the observable, super-
structural features of a particular form of society (Keat
and Urry, 1975). Again, Humeans reject the invocation of
invisible powers, and instead concentrate on establishing
regularities between observables.

To conclude my discussion in this chapter of the relation
between laws and explanation: in the positivist, conception
of explanation embodies in the D-N schema, it is the
deductive requirement – that the explanans entails the
explanandum – that ensures that the explanans explains
the explanandum event in the sense that the explanans
excludes the possibility of the non-occurrence of the
explanandum event, and it is the covering law requirement
– that the explanans includes at least one law – that

guarantees the fulfilment of the deductive requirement (Donagan, 1964). In the positivist$_{10}$ conception of explanation, it is causal connections between events that ensure that phenomena are explained. The discussion in this chapter of the problems involved in specifying how laws guarantee the deductive requirement, in characterising the nature of causality, and in attempting to identify laws empirically, raises the question of whether laws *are* necessary for explanation in the sciences in general and in sociology in particular. It is to a consideration of this issue that I turn in the next chapter.

5
Theory and Evidence

Positivism$_9$ gives laws a central place in scientific explanation but it is noticeable that many sociological explanations do not explicitly refer to laws. Homans (1964) argues that this is not because laws are not necessary, but because these explanations are what Hempel (1965a) describes as elliptically formulated, in which the laws on which they implicitly rely are so familiar from our everyday lives that it would be tiresome to formulate them explicitly on every occasion of offering an explanation, though we can state them if required. (Homans has in mind such laws as 'the more rewarding men find the results of an action, the more likely they are to take that action': Homans, 1964, p. 968.) Alternatively, the proposed sociological explanations might be no more than explanation sketches (Hempel, 1942), that is, no more than broad outlines of the direction in which future research will perhaps reveal more clearly the laws that are operating.

Both these suggestions, however, assume that the D-N account captures the essence of natural scientific explanatory (and predictive) activity and then offer excuses for sociologists' failure to fulfil the D-N conditions. They are philosophically prescriptive, and they might be countered by arguing that the proposed sociological explanations are adequate without reference to laws, and it is the covering law requirement of the D-N schema that is deficient, not the explanations. But this is just one among a number of suggestions that arise once it is recognised that there is a more profound philosophical difficulty to be faced in insisting that laws are necessary for explanation, which goes beyond demanding explicit reference to laws in concrete explanations. The vexed question is this: are empirical laws possible? Is the covering law requirement of the D-N schema compatible with empiricism? To answer this question what is needed is a precise characterisation first of what constitutes the empirical, and secondly of how laws can be empirical.

The way in which logical positivists chose to approach both these questions was influenced by their Humean empiricism and their logicist method, that is, by their belief that the only basis of sound knowledge is the observation of discrete events and that the only way of building on this base is by following the rules of reason provided by the analytic truths of formal logic, especially *Principia* logic (Harré, 1970; Bhaskar, 1975). They thought they could avoid opinion and metaphysical speculation by resting scientific knowledge on the bedrock of experience and by excluding from knowledge any contribution by the knower beyond the manipulation of what is given in experience according to the precisely specified rules of logic.

THE EMPIRICAL BASE

As described in Chapter 3, the logical positivists initially favoured the phenomenalist analysis of the empirical foundation of knowledge, which Mach took from Hume. On the phenomenalist view, what is given incorrigibly in experience is knowledge of sensations, of appearances rather than of material objects. As Mill put it, matter is the permanent possibility of sensations, and it is on the actualisation of some of these possibilities that an object is said to be perceived. In other words, what we call objects are constructions out of appearances, and our knowledge of objects, being indirect, is liable to error. We can be quite certain that we are sensing a given shape, colour, odour, and so on, but we can and do make mistakes in aggregating these and calling a collection of them an apple or a ball or an illusion.

But the difficulty in following Hume is that sense perceptions are private to the observer, and if they are thought of
as ideas, phenomenalism can give way to subjective
idealism, where physical objects are deemed unreal, the
only reality being minds and the objects of consciousness.
From this it is a short step to solipsism, where my own
mind is the only existent and all else, including what I refer
to as the physical world, is the content of my own consciousness. Mach believed he could ward off these consequences by identifying the ultimate existents as elements of
sensations – for which Russell and Moore popularised the
name 'sense-data' – such as colours, sounds, tastes, and so
on. On this account, both minds and physical objects are
arbitrary aggregates of elements of sensations, and neither
the mental nor the material is reducible to the other.

The logical positivists, wishing to avoid the traditional
metaphysical debates involved in attempting to decide
whether the ultimate existents are ideas, material objects,
or elements of sensations or whatever, turned instead to
the question of the most appropriate descriptive language
in which to unify the sciences, since they believed that
language use entailed no ontological commitment. Indeed,
they came to prefer the name 'logical empiricism' to
describe their world view, as they felt that 'logical positivism' was associated with the misunderstanding that what
Mach was proposing was a subjective idealist ontology
(Feigl, 1969b).

Initially, under the influence of Mach and Russell,
Carnap (1928) chose the phenomenalistic language because
it captured what was immediately given in experience and
therefore most certain: for example, 'there is a high-
pitched sound in my aural field'. But Neurath, drawn to
Marx's materialism and therefore opposed to the idealist
flavour of phenomenalism, preferred physicalism, where
sentences about sense-data are analysable into sentences
about the publicly observable properties of physical
objects: for example, 'this object is emitting a high-pitched
noise'. Carnap (1934) too came to adopt this view, for
although it relinquishes the incorrigibility guaranteed by

phenomenalism, it has the advantage of intersubjectivity: different observers can come to an agreement as to which physicalist sentence truthfully describes the observables in question. Physicalism, therefore, avoids the two main objections to phenomenalism. The first of these maintains that phenomenalism is internally incoherent, since we cannot talk meaningfully about private sensations unless they are first given meaning by reference to some inter-subjectively available physical object (Wittgenstein, 1953). The second main objection submits that phenomenalism is undesirable since it replaces what are normally understood as intersubjectively testable assertions about publicly available objects by contentious hypotheses about people's private experiences (Austin, 1962).

Physicalism is not free of difficulties of its own, however. For example, it does not solve but evades and so leaves unanswered the problem that phenomenalism directly confronts: what is the relation between experienced appearances and the external physical world? Also, what exactly the physicalist basis is remains unclear. Carnap (1936–7) writes of the 'thing-language' in which observable properties are ascribed to ordinary things like pencils and pianos, but these are too gross to provide a unifying empirical foundation for science, and he also writes of observable properties ascribed to space-time points: for example, 'at this space-time point a high-pitched noise is being emitted'. This opens up the difficult question of the relation between space-time points and the familiar things of ordinary life (and also the non-spatio-temporal parts of the language of physics) and an objection analogous to the second main one against pheno-menalism becomes apposite: physicalism replaces asser-tions about ordinary objects by unclear hypotheses about micro-regions of perception (Goodman, 1963). Moreover, despite the work of Neurath (1931a), Carnap (1932b), Hempel (1935) and Ayer (1967), it remains persistently contentious whether the physicalist language, whatever it is, can provide a basis on which to construct descriptions of human actions and interactions, for physicalism does seem to entail some form of behaviourism, from which one of the subject matters of interest to sociology – the intentionality of action – has been excluded (Levison, 1974). In other words, the logical empiricist sociologist is doubly disadvantaged: not only are there perhaps insurmountable difficulties in locating an appropriate language in which to describe the empirical basis of science, but also even if such a language were located, it might be impossible to capture some important sociological phenomena in it.

Carnap emphasised from the beginning that it is a matter of choice which of the alternative languages is taken as the basis on which to construct scientific knowledge. The language is chosen that best fulfils whatever purpose lies behind the attempt to identify the empirical basis of knowledge. This relaxation of empiricism, whereby what is taken as the foundation is selected not because it is the foundation, but because it is convenient so to take it, is most dramatically illustrated in the recent work of Hempel (1970), who limits himself to discussing the relation between scientific knowledge (in particular, scientific theories) and the 'antecedently understood' language or vocabulary. This is far removed from Hume's trenchant empiricism, and it illustrates how weakened the original formulation of positivism$_2$ has become. The early optimism that science could be secured on a sound foundation of experience, that it would be limited to the description of what is indubitably experienced and so be clearly demarcated from unsound metaphysical speculation, has faded under the searching analysis to which empiricism has been subject, not least by the logical positivists themselves.

EMPIRICAL STATUS OF LAWS

Even if the problem of specifying precisely what constitutes the empirical foundation of knowledge could be solved, the question remains of whether there is available an adequate characterisation of the empirical status of laws, or more generally of the relation between theory and evidence. There are three broad directions, not entirely independent, in which such a characterisation has been sought. One attempts to show how laws are established inductively from evidence. Another attempts to show that laws have deductive consequences which accord with the evidence. The third attempts to show that laws are deductively interrelated into a theoretical system which is, as a whole, somehow connected to evidence.

Inductivism

According to the tradition that goes back to Francis Bacon (1561–1626), the forerunner of British empiricism, science proceeds by the accumulation of systematic observations of particular phenomena, either naturally occurring or experimentally produced, followed eventually by the induction of general laws to fit all the observed facts. (It would, however, be a mistake to think that Bacon was an inductivist only: see Losee, 1972.) This inductivist theory of scientific method is sometimes taken as a broad characterisation of positivism, and so provides another conception of positivism, the eleventh.

There is a problem with induction, though, first posed by Hume: although it is clear that observing A_1 co-occurring (or covarying) with B_1, A_2 with B_2, and so on, licenses the inference that all observed A are B, it is not self-evident that accumulating singular observations of co-occurrence (or covariation) directly justifies our accepting the truth of the unrestricted universal law that all A are B. This has consequences for the logical positivists, for they require laws for sound explanations, but if laws cannot be conclusively verified by experience then they are meta-physical according to the principle of verifiability.

There are a variety of strategies that might be adopted in the face of this problem of induction. First, one might attempt to solve the problem by finding some justification for accepting as true the conclusions of inductive infer-ences to laws, or alternatively one could dissolve the problem by revealing somehow that it is a pseudo-problem. Secondly, one could weaken or abandon the principle of verifiability as one's specification of empiricism. Thirdly, one could modify the D-N account of explanation and prediction so that it no longer relied on unrestricted universal laws, but on empirical generalisations of scope no greater than their observed instances or on probability statements instead. Lastly, one could abandon the Baconian inductivist conceptions of scientific method and maintain that induction has no part to play in scientific inquiry.

In the first of these strategies, induction is considered to be in need of justification because it is argued that it is deficient compared with deduction. In valid deductive inferences, premisses conclusively support conclusions (that is, entail them) whereas in inductive inferences they do not. Valid deductions are truth-transmitting, whereas sound inductions are only likelihood-transmitting.

J. S. Mill did not accept the superiority of deductive over inductive arguments. He maintained that the only real inferences are inductive, from particular experiences to a general proposition, or from one particular to another. Deductions merely produce verbal transformations, re-statements in a different form of what is already known, whereas real inferences always involve going beyond what is already known to something new. Consequently, Mill argued that unrestricted universal propositions, such as those of pure mathematics and logic, *are* justified induc-tively on past experience and need no further justification. These propositions, Mill maintained, are empirical gener-alisations and they have been subject to innumerable tests and no exceptions to them have been found. Therefore we are justified in accepting their empirical truth. One such inductively justified unrestricted universal is the principle of the uniformity of nature embodied, for example, in Hume's claim that the future resembles the past, which might be stated more fully as 'all uniformities observed hitherto will continue to obtain everywhere and for ever'. Mill also maintained that laws of science can be inductively justified, even though they are not unrestricted universals in the sense that the propositions of mathematics and logic are. This is achieved by adding the uniformity principle to a set of singular statements describing the co-occurrence of A and B, which, in effect, repairs the formerly deficient inductive argument to the scientific law 'all A are B' by converting it into a deductive one. By deploying the uniformity principle in this way, Mill's famous inductive methods for discovering scientific laws and proving their truth become deductive procedures for eliminating non-causal antecedents from a finite list of possible causes (Mill, 1843, bk III, ch. 8). The four methods – Mill's fifth, the joint method of agreement and difference is the combination of the first two – are summarised in Table 5.1. (The conclu-

Table 5.1   *Mill's Methods*

	Antecedent	Consequent	
Method of Agreement:			
instance 1	ABC	XYZ	therefore A is
instance 2	ADE	XVW	the cause of X
Method of Difference:			
instance 1	ABC	XYZ	therefore A is
instance 2	BC	YZ	the cause of X
Method of Residues:			
instance 1	ABC	XYZ	
by employing the other		A is the cause of X	therefore C is
methods in other instances			the cause of Z
it is known that		B is the cause of Y	
Method of Concomitant Variations:			
instance 1	A_1BC	X_1YZ	therefore A
instance 2	A_2BC	X_2YZ	and X are
			causally related

(Where A_1 and A_2 are different magnitudes of A, and X_1 and X_2 are different magnitudes of X.)

Source: Losee, 1972, p. 149.

sion in each method needs to be modified if one allows for the complications that Mill introduced, and consequently takes the antecedents to be inus conditions, as described in Chapter 4.) Mill's methods provide the rules of inference that lie behind the application of multivariate statistics to social data in the attempt to disentangle causal relations between variables from accidental generalisations as, for example, in Lazarsfeld's elaboration techniques to uncover spurious correlations or masking.

The methods' success in deductively justifying the empirical truth of laws depends on two conditions. The first requires that all possible relevant rival antecedents are known and have been eliminated so that, for example, in the method of concomitant variations one can be confident that the covariation of A and X is not a spurious correlation. Secondly, the truth of the additional premiss – the uniformity principle (of which Mill's version is the law of sufficient causation, according to which every consequent is invariably and unconditionally the effect of one antecedent or of one set of antecedents) – being itself an empirical proposition, must be justified. In accordance with his radical inductivism, Mill argued inductively that past experience establishes that both conditions are fulfilled. Invariable laws *have* been discovered by examining limited ranges of antecedents and consequents, and past observations of regularities do justify the law of causation. But, following Hume's original formulation of the problem of induction, objectors counter that Mill's appeal to induction to demonstrate the truth of the two conditions required for the success of his inductive methods is circular, for the new inductions themselves rely on additional premisses that are versions of the conclusions they purport to demonstrate. Past evidence supports the uniformity principle only if the future resembles the past, that is, only if the uniformity principle is true. Moreover, in addition to begging the question, Mill's inductive justification of the premisses required to deductively justify (or prove the truth of) causal laws would seem also to be empirically unsupported, since our experiences of novelties commonly violate previous regularities.

In view of this alleged circularity and empirical falsity of Mill's justification of induction, and because his radical empiricism has fallen into disfavour (see Chapter 3), another way of justifying induction by reconstructing it as deduction has been tried. This approach, introduced by John Maynard Keynes (1883–1946), turns from trying to bolster the premisses to diluting the conclusion instead (Keynes, 1921). It involves converting the conclusion of an inductive inference into a probability statement. This strategy, in effect, concedes that the problem of induction cannot be solved unless the principle of verifiability is weakened. No longer is it required that experience conclusively verify laws before they are considered scientific rather than metaphysical. Instead, all that is required is that, as Ayer (1946) put it, experience render laws probable. It is this tradition that provides the justification for sociological research in which information is collected by means of sample surveys and then inductive statistics are used to estimate with what degree of confidence or at what level of statistical significance – in other words, with what probability – it can be said that laws about the population are true given the evidence of the sample.

Attention then centres on explicating the notion of probability. Initially, logical positivists preferred the frequency theory of probability, because according to this theory probability statements are empirical statements describing the number of times some event has happened relative to the number of times it might have happened (Reichenbach, 1938; von Mises, 1928; the modern, propensity theory of probability is closely related to the frequency theory: Kyburg, 1974). For example, if it is observed over the years that a steady 11% of 18-year-olds in Britain attend university, then there is an 11% probability of 18-year-olds in Britain going to university in the current year. But there are difficulties with the frequency theory when considering unbounded series of events: for example, to avoid being misled by short-run variations, such as the university attendance rate of 18-year-olds in Britain during the Second World War, it is necessary to define probability as the limit to which the frequency tends in the long run. Immediately the problem of induction reappears as the problem of trying to estimate the long run or limiting frequency from a finite run. The uniformity principle has to be invoked: if the future resembles the (recent) past, then there will be an 11% probability of 18-year-olds in Britain going to university. Without the uniformity principle, an observed relative frequency in a finite run is compatible with *any* limiting frequency, depending on what events happen in the future. Attempts to predict the age participation rate – the percentage of 18-year-olds wishing to go to university – so as to be able to plan the appropriate size of the universities in Britain illustrate this problem (DES, 1978).

Some logical positivists, most notably Carnap (1945), recognising this problem with the frequency theory, turned to an alternative conception of probability in which it is a logical relation between evidence and a conclusion, like entailment but weaker. This view of probability was developed by Carnap (1950) into confirmation theory, where the aim is to provide a logic of induction, precise rules for calculating the support or degree of confirmation that a particular set of evidence propositions give a particular conclusion. Despite the sophistication of Carnap's confirmation theory, it faces two related difficulties. First, because a proposition might be confirmed by one set of evidence statements but disconfirmed by other sets, the confirmationist must insist upon the requirement of total evidence before calculating the degree of confirmation of the proposition. It is no more certain that this condition can be fulfilled than can the similar one on which the success of Mill's eliminative methods of induction depends – that all relevant rival antecedents be taken into consideration (Hempel, 1965a). Secondly, Carnap's system of inductive logic assigns a probability of zero to scientific laws formulated as unrestricted generalisations, regardless of the evidence available, since no finite amount of evidence can confirm such generalisations of potentially infinite scope.

Even if modern developments in confirmation theory overcame these difficulties (Hintikka, 1968) and it were possible to assign a non-zero probability to laws which successfully specified their degree of confirmation on the basis of all available evidence, this approach to solving the problem of induction requires that the D-N account of explanation and prediction be modified so that it no longer relies on universal laws (all A are B) but only on probability statements (it is 90% probable that A are B). Hempel (1965a) describes an appropriately modified schema of what he calls inductive-statistical (I-S) explanations, which is summarised in Figure 5.1. (This representation of the I-S schema differs somewhat from Hempel, 1965a, p. 383, but it makes clearer the relation between the I-S schema and the D-N schema portrayed in Chapter 4. Hempel also describes a third, deductive-statistical (D-S) schema, in which statistical or probability laws are explained by deducing them from premises containing other statistical laws.)

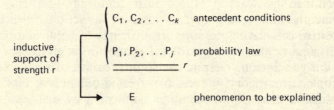

Figure 5.1   *The inductive-statistical schema.*

Although Hempel refers to I-S arguments as explanations, probabilistic laws cannot be used to explain or predict the occurrence of singular states of affairs. However large the probability r is, if it is less than 100% then it remains unclear whether the state of affairs described in the explanandum sentence is one for which being A is associated with being B or whether it is one for which being A is not associated with being B.

Some authors, persuaded by the difficulties encountered in attempting to justify induction deductively (either with Mill by adding a uniformity principle or with Carnap by turning to probability theory), suggest that it is more appropriate to offer a pragmatic justification. This sort of solution was originally offered by Peirce (1883) and later developed by Reichenbach (1949) and Salmon (1961). According to this strategy, the adoption of inductive procedures is justified as a means to the scientific end of producing an accumulating body of universal laws. Inductive principles cannot be validated (demonstratively proved) but they can be 'vindicated' by the success of scientific research (Feigl, 1952). Induction is a rule of the scientific game. If scientists use it, and if the world is organised according to universal laws, then they might discover those laws. If they do not use induction, however, then they deny themselves even the possibility of discovering universal laws. If they use it and the world is not organised according to laws but is chaotic, then no rules will be applicable and the user of induction will be no more disadvantaged than any other person.

(It is in a similar way that some have sought to justify the principle of verifiability. If it is to be acceptable to logical positivists as part of science, the principle must be analytically true or empirically true. But it is not a tautology, and if it is taken to be an empirical statement describing how people use the term 'meaning', it seems to be false, since not all people say that metaphysics is meaningless. In other words, being neither analytically nor empirically true, it seems to be a candidate for rejection as metaphysical. To avoid this, Ayer, 1959, argues that it is a linguistic entity of another sort: it is a convention or rule, used to deflate the claims of metaphysics by revealing that metaphysical inquiries do not produce analyses of reality more profound than those of empirical science, for the results of such inquiries are not descriptive of the world at all. Using the principle as a rule therefore concentrates effort on analysing science.)

Critics of the pragmatic justification of induction argue that it provides no epistemological criteria for discriminating between good and bad inductions. It justifies all inductions equally and consequently gives no guide for the practice of science, for the choice of laws (Black, 1954).

If this criticism cannot be met, then it appears that all the various attempts to solve the problem of induction are unsatisfactory. An alternative response to the problem is, then, to sidestep all the difficulties that arise in the attempted solutions by arguing that the demand for a general justification is based on a misunderstanding of induction. This dissolves the problem: inductive inferences are reasonable and justified, and those who assert that they are not are violating ordinary linguistic uses of the terms 'reasonable' and 'justified' (Strawson, 1952), in a similar manner to those who insist that 'cause' is ordinarily unintelligible and requires analysis. After collecting a large number of reports of the co-occurrence and co-absence of A and B, one has good reason for, and is justified in, asserting that any A will be a B, rather than, for example, that any A will not be a B. To insist otherwise might be formally correct within the ideal language of deductive logic, but that runs counter to our ordinary language, to our ordinary way of establishing scientific laws.

The advantage of this approach is that it frees scientists from all philosophers' post-Hume worries about the empirical status of laws conceived of as the products of inductive inferences. But the disadvantage is that in leaving induction as an unanalysable primitive, like the pragmatic justification of induction, it provides practising scientists with no criteria for distinguishing between good and bad inductions, reasonable and unreasonable arguments and explanations, other than their own unexplicated intuitions. Science then, the positivist$_2$ fears, is freed from empirical control and open to individual or collective caprice.

Deductivism

Perhaps the problems involved in all attempts to account satisfactorily for induction show that the problem of induction is insoluble, and that the Baconian inductivist conception of scientific method must be abandoned in favour of an analysis of science that recognises deduction as the only form of legitimate inference. This approach, although suggested by many authors, has been most fully exploited by Karl Popper (1902–), a native of Vienna who communicated closely with several logical positivists although he did not formally associate himself with the Vienna Circle, largely because he rejected their principle of verifiability, and also because he felt the logicistic method had little to contribute to the central question of the philosophy of science, which for him was the growth of scientific knowledge (Popper, 1978). Popper took the insolubility of the problem of induction as grounds for rejecting the idea that science is demarcated from metaphysics by virtue of science's inductive method, that is, by the discovery and verification of laws by inducing them from observational and experimental evidence. For Popper, it is a mistake to dismiss metaphysics as meaningless, as the logical positivists did. The important distinction is not between verifiable science and nonsensical metaphysics, but between science and pseudo-science, the distinguishing feature of science being its openness to critical appraisal, made possible by the falsifiability of its laws (Popper, 1934, 1963).

Popper's conception of science is founded upon the asymmetry between verifiability and falsifiability. Although innumerable instances of As that are Bs cannot demonstrate the truth of the law all A are B, one single observation of an A that is not a B conclusively shows that the law is false. Science, in Popper's view, proceeds by trial and error, by the familiar hypothetico-deductive (H-D) method, which involves conjecturing hypothetical laws, deducing from them observable test implications and comparing these with our experiences. If observational evidence contradicts the test implications, the hypothetical law must be rejected or modified. If, on the other hand, the evidence accords with the test implications then the hypothetical law is accepted for the present. It is of course not verified, only corroborated, as Popper says, for future tests might refute it. Induction plays no part in science according to this critical rationalist theory of scientific method, as it is known. The only inferences in science are deductive ones, from hypothesis to test implications. Hypotheses are not generated by any rational process of induction from singular co-occurrences. Their source is a psychological or sociological matter, beyond the bounds of the philosophy or logic of science, which restricts itself to analysing the justification for rejecting or retaining whatever hypotheses scientists entertain, regardless of how they come to entertain them.

The hypothetico-deductive account of scientific method is well known among sociologists and is sometimes described by them as *the* positivist method (Worsley, 1970). It provides another conception of positivism: positivism$_{12}$ is a theory of scientific method according to which science progresses by conjecturing hypotheses and attempting to refute them. It is in the H-D tradition that sociologists propose null hypotheses and use inductive statistics in the attempt to refute those hypotheses and so corroborate the alternative hypotheses.

If the H-D method were as straightforward as described in the simple account above, then few general laws would remain unfalsified, for our experiences commonly conflict with the deductive consequences of laws. All that would remain would be very restricted non-universal generalisations, hedged with conditions to exclude disconfirming instances, a dispiriting result not dissimilar to that facing a radical inductivist like Mill, given the common occurrence of novel experiences violating past uniformities. But a glance at the D-N schema presented in Figure 4.1 in the previous chapter reveals that the H-D method does not straightforwardly test a hypothesis, for test implications are deducible from a hypothetical law only in conjunction with a set of additional conditions and auxiliary hypotheses, perhaps summarised by a *ceteris paribus* clause (Duhem, 1906). Consequently, it remains uncertain whether a falsifying observation results from the falsity of the hypothesis under test or the falsity of any one of the auxiliary hypotheses or the failure to fulfil any one of the conditions. One response to this impossibility of conclusive falsification, commonly but mistakenly attributed to the French philosopher and physicist Pierre Duhem (1861–1916), is to suggest that scientists accept the auxiliary hypotheses as unfalsifiable and the antecedent conditions as fulfilled, at least for the duration of the test, so that the hypothetical law can be considered to be the only potentially falsifiable item. In other words, some hypotheses are granted the status of conventions, statements that are neither true nor false but which operate as methodological rules (rules to allow one to proceed), so that other hypotheses can be tested empirically.

The disadvantage of this conventionalist strategy is that, in the absence of empirical criteria for selecting which hypotheses are to be unfalsifiable, it enables any hypotheses to be protected from disconfirmation at the whim of the individual scientist or by agreement among a community of scientists. This might be called the problem of conventionalism, and it is the analogue for deductivism of the problem posed for inductivism by the pragmatic solution to the problem of induction.

Popper sought to avoid this disagreeable consequence of conventionalism by recommending a methodological rule, the adoption of which, he maintains, facilitates the rational growth of science. His rule is: avoid conventionalist stratagems, by which he means that one must decide to refrain from protecting the theoretical system of science by introducing *ad hoc* hypotheses, or by redefining the empirical content of concepts, or by doubting the evidence of the experimenter or theorist, and so on (Johansson, 1975). The mark of science, as opposed to pseudo-science, is its susceptibility to revision. It is dynamic and self-correcting and does not cling dogmatically to hypotheses in the face of disconfirming evidence.

Popper's methodological approach to the problem of conventionalism might be formulated in parallel terms to the pragmatic defence of induction. Hypothetico-deductivism is a rule of the scientific game and conventionalism is not. If scientists use the H-D method and avoid conventionalist stratagems, and if the world is organised according to laws, then science might progress through the elimination of refuted hypothetical laws. If scientists do not use the H-D method or do use conventionalist stratagems, however, they deny themselves even the possibility of excluding from knowledge false conjectures. Science will become dogma, protecting itself from potentially falsifying evidence behind a barrier of *ad hoc* additions. If scientists do use the H-D method and the world is not organised according to laws, then no rules will be applicable and the user of the H-D method will be no more disadvantaged than any other person.

It is Imre Lakatos (1922–74) who has developed this strand of Popper's work furthest. Lakatos (1970) attempts to specify the methodological rules used to decide which developments in a series of connected theories he calls research programmes should be rejected and which retained on the evidence of attempted refutations. The central idea is that research programmes are progressive – science progresses rationally – when each theory is successfully defeated by falsifying evidence and a new or rival theory is available that explains both the previous success of the old theory and the evidence that falsifies the old theory. In other words, the shift from theory T_1 to T_2 is progressive if T_2 explains everything that T_1 did, if T_2 makes some novel predictions that T_1 does not, and if some of these predictions have been tested and corroborated.

Lakatos's critics object that at the general level his notion of the progressiveness of a research programme is neither a necessary nor a sufficient basis on which to decide in which direction to develop scientific theorising (Suppe, 1977) and that at the specific level his methodological rules are inadequate: for example, he does not indicate how one is to prevent the *ad hoc* addition of irrelevant corroborated content (say, from biology) to a new sociological theory simply to secure the falsification of its sociological predecessor, except for the vague suggestion that the new theory must be derivable from what he calls the metaphysical hard core of the research programme, that is, the part of the system of theories that it has been decided is unfalsifiable (Glymour, 1980).

What Lakatos's proposals focus attention on is the need for a precise specification of degrees of corroboration, or conversely of falsifiability, if the problem of conventionalism is to be overcome. Any attempt to provide a measure of falsifiability in terms of the number of potential falsifiers would encounter the same difficulties facing confirmation theorists – those of requiring total evidence and of assigning, in this case, infinite falsifiability to unrestricted universals. In view of this, Popper (1934, pp. 387–419) insists that the degree of corroboration is not the number of potential tests which a theory has been subjected to and passed, and nor is it a probability for it violates the laws of the probability calculus. His argument is that the more a theory says, the more opportunity there is for finding that it conflicts with experience: the greater its empirical content, the less probable its truth. Yet the greater a theory's empirical content, the more falsifiable it is, and therefore, if it remains unrefuted, the more corroborated it is. Thus corroborability cannot be a probability and Carnap's efforts to produce a logic of induction or theory of confirmation based on probability are misdirected. But Popper does not provide a logic of corroborability to fill the gap. Moreover, critics maintain that scientists simply do not proceed by conjecturing and testing the most falsifiable and therefore least probable theories, then calling their efforts progress because countless bizarre hypotheses have been rejected. As noted above, Lakatos's move to exclude this absurdity is to require that each successive theory include the empirical content of its predecessor, but this is too restrictive, for it provides no way of comparing the falsifiability of those theories not connected by the relation of entailment or inclusion, such as the rival Marxist and relative deprivation theories of revolution. Overall, then, deductivism seems to be as unsuccessful as inductivism in providing a satisfactory account of the empirical status of scientific laws.

Theoretical Holism

When the H-D method was introduced above, the item under test was described as a hypothetical law. Popper, however, argues that it is theories rather than isolated propositions that are appraised as scientific or pseudoscientific by the H-D method and Lakatos extends this to research programmes – series of connected theories. They make this move principally to overcome the difficulty that isolated existential propositions are not falsifiable, even though they commonly feature in scientific discourse. For example, 'there are classless societies' is not refutable by the failure to observe classless societies, however assiduous one's search, for the possibility always remains that they might be observed in the future. There would be no difficulty here if one were prepared to accept verifiability as well as falsifiability as a criterion of the scientificity of propositions, for existential propositions are conclusively verifiable: the observation of one classless society verifies 'there are classless societies'. But because Popper completely rejects verifiability, his argument instead is that existential propositions need not be dismissed as pseudoscientific provided they are part of a theory that is falsifiable as a whole. This argument is not successful, however, for any sentence can be made part of some falsifiable system, so no sentences can be appraised as non-scientific. But leaving aside this formal failing, Popper's work nevertheless serves as a reminder that the logical positivists' characterisation of science as consisting only of empirical propositions and logical rules perhaps needs to be supplemented by adding the language of theory. This then raises the possibility that it is within the realm of scientific theory that a solution might be found to the problem of the empirical, and therefore scientific rather than metaphysical or pseudoscientific, status of laws. Perhaps the distinguishing feature of laws is that they are part of theory, rather than that they are induced from evidence or have deductive consequences which accord with the evidence.

Given their Humean empiricism, logical positivists refused to avail themselves of this possible solution, at least initially, for they denied any autonomy to scientific theory and attempted to make it entirely subservient to experience. They feared that theory might be metaphysics in disguise, so they took it as their task to show that theory is cognitively significant in the only way they deemed acceptable – by being connected to experience.

Indeed, they began by attempting to eliminate theory from science altogether: there is no need for theory when science is conceived of as the explanation and prediction of observables (Hempel, 1958). The principle of verifiability was designed to exclude from science and dismiss as metaphysical any statement that is not directly verifiable. As described earlier (Chapter 3), Mach's aim was to recast the whole of scientific theory in terms of descriptions of relations between elements of sensations. Mach's attempted phenomenalistic reduction encountered the difficulty that the mathematical parts of theory cannot be translated into statements about sensations without adopting the untenable radical empiricist view of Mill. To avoid this and at the same time avoid consigning mathematical theory to metaphysics, the logical positivists allowed mathematical propositions an autonomous place in scientific theory provided they were thought of as part of logic, that is, as syntactical rules for formulating and manipulating the other, empirical statements which derived their content or meaning solely from the observations they summarised.

In retaining Mach's eliminative ideal, the logical positivists argued that theoretical propositions, unless they were rules of logic or could be constructed from (or reduced to) directly verifiable propositions using the syntactical rules of logic, were to be discarded as metaphysical. This was Carnap's aim in *The Logical Structure of the World* (1928), where he sought to demonstrate that all the extra-logical non-observational terms of science could be exhaustively defined in phenomenalistic terms. Theoretical terms, on this eliminative view, are merely abbreviations for collections of phenomenalistic descriptions, and so are strictly redundant in scientific talk. Bridgman's operationalism is a less formal version of the same eliminative approach, attempting to replace theoretical predicates definitionally by descriptions of operations, and more formal versions are available in the work of various logicians, especially Frank Ramsey and William Craig (Hempel, 1965b).

Unfortunately, the eliminative approach to theory trans-
fixes the logical positivist on the horns of the dilemma that
raised its head in Chapter 4. Either theoretical laws are
empirical generalisations, in which case explanatory and
predictive success is in jeopardy unless laws can be distinguished from accidental generalisations, and Humeans
have failed to draw the required distinction in a generally
acceptable manner. Or theoretical laws have no substantive content, being analytic statements or tautologies, in
which case they cannot function as the basis of the
explanation and prediction of empirical occurrences.

Logical positivists were saved from having to solve this
dilemma by the failure of the eliminative strategy: not all
extra-logical theoretical terms used by scientists are
explicitly definable in observational terms. Even the most
trenchant critics of metaphysics recognise that scientists
make assertions employing terms not exhaustively
reducible to observational terms, which, if purged as metaphysical lapses, would leave science greatly impoverished.
In the currently popular idiom, scientific discourse is
replete with 'theory-laden' terms. Carnap (1936–7), for
example, showed that dispositional terms, like malleable or
thirsty or intelligent, cannot be explicitly defined in observational terms using *Principia* logic. Consequently, just as
the original demarcation criterion – the principle of verifiability – was relaxed, and replaced by confirmation theory,
so too the notion that theoretical terms are exhaustively
definable was replaced by the idea that they are only
partially definable: theoretical terms are accepted as non-
metaphysical provided some experiential evidence is necessary for their truth, even if that evidence is not sufficient
for their truth, in the sense that it does not exhaust the
meanings of the terms.

This move carries with it the advantage that theoretical
terms retain an 'openness of meaning' (Hempel, 1958). If a
theoretical term is explicitly defined in terms of a set of
observations then the addition of further observations to
that set redefines the theoretical term, giving it a new
meaning incompatible with the first. If, however, the term

is only partially defined so that its sense is not exhausted by the set of known observations, it remains possible to extend the range of the term by applying it to new observable occurrences that provide additional partial definitions of it. For example, 'educational attainment', if explicitly defined by measures of literacy and numeracy, takes on a new and different meaning if it is to include, additionally, the number of public examinations passed, with the consequence that theories using the term in the original sense cannot be compared with theories embodying the term with its new meaning. If, on the other hand, the definition in terms of measures of literacy and numeracy is only partial, the range of application of 'educational attainment' can be expanded to new contexts, such as passing exams or breadth of knowledge or verbal fluency, each of which provides a supplementary partial definition of 'educational attainment', and so old and new theories containing the term can be compared.

Even the weakened, partial definition relation between theory and evidence is too restrictive, however, for it cannot satisfactorily accommodate metrical theoretical concepts like length and velocity (Hempel, 1958). One response was to take this difficulty as an indication that the restriction of logic to that of the *Principia* should be abandoned and that stronger logical concepts and principles should be introduced. For example, material implication might be supplemented by the addition of modal operators or irreducible causal predicates – the extensional 'if . . ., then . . .' supplemented by the modal counterpart 'if . . ., then with causal necessity . . .'.

An alternative response was to further weaken the principle of verifiability, and this was favoured by logical positivists because it was felt that the stronger logics required by the first response were obscure. Attempts to specify the empirical significance of theoretical terms one by one were abandoned in favour of the idea that it is a theoretical system as a whole which must, at some points only, be related to the observational language by some form of partial definitions, usually referred to as correspondence rules (Feigl, 1970). This concedes that theoretical terms are ineliminable not just because those that do connect with experiential evidence through correspondence rules are only partially defined by that evidence, but also because many of the terms in the theoretical system are not part of any correspondence rules at all.

This is an extremely attenuated form of empiricism that considerably erodes the idea that empirical science might be clearly demarcated from metaphysics. A system of propositions becomes scientific as soon as some (or even one?) of its theoretical terms are (is) connected to experience by correspondence rules, and thereby at least partially defined by observation terms. The remaining theoretical terms – those that are not part of the correspondence rules – have only whatever empirical content seeps into them by virtue of their being connected (however indirectly) by theoretical postulates to the partially defined theoretical term(s). Given that any term can be attached by postulate to a theoretical system, no term can be found metaphysical. What started as a rigorous attempt to exclude metaphysics by firmly connecting each part of theory to experience ends by allowing the whole system of theory to float away and merge into the metaphysical atmosphere and yet retain the title science provided only that it is tenuously anchored to the bedrock of experience by perhaps as few as one correspondence rule that only partly defines (one of) its terms.

The urgent question then is whether this outcome can be prevented by finding some restriction that can be put on the terms that may appear in theory. To answer this, one needs to consider the source both of the meaning of the empirically uninterpreted theoretical terms and of the remainder of the meaning of the theoretical terms that are only partially defined in observation terms. The logical positivists, unable to locate an acceptable way of construing theory as a system of empirical generalisations interrelated by the language of *Principia* logic, and unwilling either to extend their logic or to grant that there is any source of cognitive significance beyond that given by experience, were drawn to an instrumentalist interpretation of theories. On this view, uneliminable theoretical laws are neither true nor false, nor tautological. Instead they are another sort of sentence: they are conventions, convenient but meaningless calculating devices or instruments that are necessary for explanation and prediction in the sense that they license inferences from one set of observation statements (the explanans) to another (the explanandum) (Ryle, 1949).

For the logical positivist, however, instrumentalism has two deficiencies. First, although it offers a solution to the empiricists' dilemma over the status of scientific laws, it nevertheless abandons the D-N conception of explanation and prediction, for conclusions about the world are not deduced from the instrumental laws but are drawn in accordance with them or inferred as applications of them (Toulmin, 1953, ch. 3). Secondly, as with the pragmatist solution to the problem of induction and the conventionalist strand of hypothetico-deductivism, the choice of instrument or theory is left open to the individual or collective whim of scientists. Instrumentalists attempt to meet this latter complaint by offering non-empiricist criteria for selecting between alternative theories, such as their economy or elegance or plausibility or utility in effecting the transition between observation statements. But it is doubtful whether these criteria can be applied self-consistently, for each can itself be only a convenient instrument and must therefore be revisable at will, unless some empiricist foundation were smuggled into the chosen criterion to provide an objective basis on which to compare alternative theoretical instruments. Such contraband would be to no avail, however, for it was the failure of empiricist criteria that prompted the move to instrumentalism in the first place.

Despite these deficiencies, logical positivists prefer instrumentalism to the alternative, realist interpretation of scientific theories, according to which theoretical terms describe the properties and powers of real objects, structures and processes, even though these may be observationally inaccessible. In other words, for realists there is an additional source of cognitive significance beyond experience: the extra-logical non-observational terms of scientific theory have meaning by virtue of having a real referent, even if that referent is unobservable. Correspondence rules, on this view, describe the circumstances in which the real entities and structures described by theoretical terms manifest themselves to experience. Correspondence rules are empirically meaningful propositions, in sharp contrast both with the early logical positivist view where the correspondence rules are analytic – formal syntactical rules – and with the instrumentalist view where the correspondence rules are no more than conventional stipulations.

Just as the realist interpretation of necessity offered a solution to the Humeans' difficulties with causation, so too the realist interpretation of theories offers an attractive solution to the problem of the status of laws required for D-N explanations: laws describe the workings of real objects and structures in the world. They describe the underlying generative mechanisms that are responsible for the observed features of the world. But given that these mechanisms are only partially defined by their observational manifestations, the problem facing the realist is how to place limits on their introduction or, in other words, how to choose between alternative theories about the underlying reality. Like the instrumentalist, appeals might be made to elegance, plausibility, utility and effectiveness in explaining and predicting, but there is one additional criterion available to the realist that is not available to the instrumentalist: postulated theories make existence claims about the mechanisms they describe. This turns attention from discovering and testing laws, however they are construed, to postulating mechanisms and attempting to demonstrate that they exist (Harré, 1961).

In the eyes of logical positivists this redirection of attention is a failing of realism, for the role of the D-N schema is downgraded: deducing the explanandum from an explanans describing the working of a mechanism becomes a minor part of science compared with investigating the existence claims of the mechanism. And a second failing of realism is that although it offers a solution to empiricist's dilemma over the status of scientific laws, by making the central feature of science the speculative postulation of hidden mechanisms to explain observed occurrences, it raises all the problems that motivated the anti-meta-physical, empiricist programme of the early positivists in the first place.

In sum: logical positivist philosophers found that by responding to the challenges posed by problems within their programme they either moved towards conventionalist solutions or were forced back to realist positions. In both cases, certain key features of their conception of science, such as causality and laws, escaped from the court of experience, either by becoming mere convenient stipulations, useful devices for patterning appearances, or by disappearing out of the reach of experience, to be glimpsed only darkly through manifestations of their workings.

Conclusion

In the foregoing pages I have identified twelve positivisms. Positivism$_1$ is a theory of history in which improvements in knowledge are both the motor of progress and the source of social stability (Comte$_1$). Positivism$_2$ is a theory of knowledge according to which the only kind of sound knowledge available to humankind is that of science grounded in observation (Comte$_2$). Positivism$_3$ is a unity of science thesis according to which all sciences can be integrated into a single natural system (Comte$_3$). Positivism$_4$ is a secular religion of humanity devoted to the worship of society (Comte$_4$). Positivism$_5$ is a theory of history in which the motor of progress that guarantees the emergence of superior forms of society is competition between increasingly differentiated individuals (Spencer). Positivism$_6$ is a theory of knowledge according to which the natural science of sociology consists of the collection and statistical analysis of quantitative data about society (Durkheim). Positivism$_7$ is a theory of meaning, combining phenomenalism and logicistic method, and captured by the principle of verifiability, according to which the meaning of a proposition consists in its method of verification (logical positivism$_1$). Positivism$_8$ is a programme for the unification of the sciences both syntactically and semantically (logical positivism$_2$). Positivism$_9$ is a theory of knowledge according to which science consists of a corpus of interrelated, true, simple, precise and wide-ranging universal laws that are central to explanation and prediction in the manner described in the D-N schema (Hempel). Positivism$_{10}$ is a theory of knowledge according to which science consists of a corpus of causal laws on the basis of which phenomena are explained and predicted. Positivism$_{11}$ is a theory of scientific method according to which science progresses by inducing laws from observational and experimental evidence (Bacon). Positivism$_{12}$ is a theory of scientific method according to which science progresses by conjecturing hypotheses and attempting to refute them, so that false conjectures are eliminated and corroborated ones retained (Popper).

These positivisms are different proposals as to what is to be understood by the term 'positivism', supported by different individuals or groups at different times. Some now have an old-fashioned air, especially the religion, positivism$_4$. The two theories of history, positivism$_1$ (also known as scientism) and positivism$_5$ (sometimes referred to as social evolutionism), are unrelated to the epistemological theses, positivisms$_{2,3,6-12}$, except by historical contingency. Both face potent challenges from Marx's work and developments out of it.

Positivism$_2$ is identical with traditional empiricism: positive (as opposed to theological and metaphysical) knowledge *is* empirical knowledge, which is the only sound (or scientific) knowledge because observation (or more generally, experience) is the only sound source of knowledge. This view of knowledge is challenged by those who maintain there are alternative sources of sound or scientific knowledge, such as the traditional rationalists, for whom reason provides indubitable truths about the world. It might be that some contemporary sociologists – the French structuralists, perhaps – espouse this rationalist view. Empiricism is challenged also by the dialectical view of knowledge, according to which the only source of sound knowledge is praxis, action in and on the world through which we come to know the world at the same time as we change it. This view has found support in sociology among Hegelian-Marxists.

Positivism$_2$ was extended by the logical positivists, to make science consist not only of empirical knowledge but also of analytic truths, which gave a place in science to mathematics and logic. Positivism$_7$, the principle of verifiability, was employed by the logical positivists in an attempt to justify their extended positivism$_2$: all science, consisting only of meaningful propositions, is verifiable by empirical or logical means. Pragmatism and operationalism are further attempts to justify positivism$_2$.

Positivism$_2$, in both its traditional empiricist and extended logical positivist forms, is intended to include the social sciences: all sound *social* knowledge is empirical (or empirical and analytic). Positivism$_2$, then, forms a basis for the unity of science thesis, positivism$_3$ (also known as naturalism). Positivism$_8$ is the logical positivists' linguistic version of the unity of science thesis, and it restates their commitment to their extended positivism$_2$: all science employs the same observational vocabulary manipulated by the same formal language of relations. Critics argue either that there are alternative bases for the unification of the sciences, other than empiricism and logicism, or that the sciences are not unified because, for example, there are alternative sources of social, as opposed to physical, knowledge, such as introspection or *verstehen*. The positivist$_2$ counter-arguments are either that these (only apparently) alternative sources provide knowledge of the same type of phenomena of awareness as external sensory perception (Mach's elements of sensation), or that these alternative sources, while different, are only suggestive of hypotheses which still have to be verified in the usual empiricist ways before they become knowledge (Abel, 1948).

Positivism$_{11}$ (inductivism) and positivism$_{12}$ (hypothetico-deductivism) amplify positivism$_2$ by describing two different ways in which scientific laws and theories are to be related to experience. Positivism$_6$ is a specification of the way in which positivism$_2$ (amplified as either positivism$_{11}$ or positivism$_{12}$) should apply to sociology. It insists that the empirical base be described quantitatively and that hypothetical laws be tested (verified or corroborated) statistically. But the relation between positivism$_2$ and positivism$_6$ is not a necessary one: sociologists who are opposed to quantification and statistics but nevertheless sympathetic to positivism$_2$, such as the nineteenth-century social philosophers and some twentieth-century symbolic interactionists, in effect propose specifications of positivism$_2$ different from positivism$_6$, that is, non-statistical ways of relating sociological theories to evidence.

Positivism$_9$ and positivism$_{10}$, although popular characterisations of positivism, can be reconciled with positivism$_2$ only by adopting attenuated conceptions of law and cause, or by curtailing the constraint that experience imposes on science which lies at the heart of positivism$_2$, as described in Chapters 4 and 5. Positivism$_9$ and positivism$_{10}$ are challenged by those sociologists who maintain that social phenomena must be explained teleologically, in terms of intentional goals or ends. This claim underlies the variety of functionalism that threatens to divorce sociology from the physical sciences, whose subject matter, it is argued, does not have goals in the same sense. The positivist$_9$ and positivist$_{10}$ responses are either to dismiss appeals to ends as metaphysical (as Comte did) or to attempt to show that teleological explanations involve no more than a system of interacting causal relationships featuring a negative-feedback loop; in other words, that functional laws are a variety of causal law, that teleological explanations are a form of positivist$_9$ explanation.

PHILOSOPHY

Twentieth-century philosophers of science have devoted an enormous amount of attention to working out the details of the epistemological positivisms, and these explicative efforts have revealed severe internal difficulties. Attempts to solve these difficulties have led in two directions. Either they have pushed towards various forms of conventionalism, where crucial features of positivist conceptions of science such as its empirical base, laws, causes and theories are thought of as being agreements among scientists, decided upon to allow them to continue constructing an (apparently) objective and coherent system of science. Or they have pulled back towards realism, where the crucial features of science are thought of as manifestations of ontologically real structures and processes which are only partly revealed to experience but which guarantee the objectivity of science.

What the internal dynamics of twentieth-century positivism suggest, then, is that conventionalism and realism are continuous with developments in the positivist programme formulated by the logical positivists. Those who take the contrary view that the three philosophies of science are discontinuous and opposed alternatives, and in particular those who take this view as part of their argument that it is realism and not positivism that captures the essence of natural and social science (Harré, 1970; Benton, 1977), commonly rest their case on vignettes of episodes drawn from the history or current practice of science. However, whether these studies of scientific work can demonstrate the truth of one of the philosophical pictures of science or the falsity of the other two is questionable. It is undoubtedly the case that the preference for a particular philosophy of science is influenced in some way by contemporary scientific work: think of the influence of biology on Comte and Spencer, physics on the logical positivists, and Marxism, with its attribution of real interests to groups of people, on recent realists (Bhaskar, 1975, 1979). Yet it is unlikely that the *whole* of scientific activity is characterised by those features that one philosophy of science identifies as central, for example, the quest for laws in positivism[9], the formation of agreements among scientists in conventionalism, or the postulation of generative mechanisms in realism. Consequently, whether the episodes or the branches of science examined are representative is a crucial issue, as is the question of the relation between philosophers' reconstructions of scientific activity and the actual practices of scientists (McMullin, 1970). In particular, against the arguments of the realists, it might be noted that the early twentieth-century positivists were in several cases practising scientists who believed that their philosophy of science accurately represented their scientific work, and the same is true of the early conventionalist Duhem.

Whereas it is easy nowadays to mobilise support for the rejection of simple characterisations of positivism, it is worth remembering that the grounds for such a rejection were largely worked out within the positivist programme itself. Simple characterisations of positivism are, however, in no worse straits than either conventionalism or realism characterised with equal simplicity. The temptation to abandon positivism entirely because thorough and detailed analyses have revealed its flaws, and adopt instead relatively unanalysed alternatives which might in the end turn out to be no less seriously flawed, should perhaps be resisted.

This resistance must not, however, lapse into complacent dogmatism. The initial impetus of *philosophie positive* in the nineteenth century was freedom: freedom of human reason from external authority, from religion, from tradition. But positivism$_2$ imposed its own unfreedom when it demanded that reason submit to experience, to the given. It is this constraint, this alignment of knowledge with the status quo, that the Frankfurt school found so limiting in the positivist epistemological programme (Marcuse, 1941). Positivists of all kinds must not forget their roots. They must temper their preference for objectivity and rigorous systematisation with the spirit of critique, of open evaluation. They must be willing to judge the facts they carefully document and painstakingly analyse. In so doing, they must recapture Comte's first formulation: improvements in knowledge must be made to serve humankind.

SOCIOLOGY

The debates over the rival merits of positivist, conventionalist and realist pictures of science have been actively joined by philosophers of the social sciences (Keat and Urry, 1975). Many sociologists, too, have been bewitched by the developments and changes in philosophers' analyses and understandings of explanation, experience, causality, laws and theory reviewed in the last two chapters, and they have responded by adopting a whole spectrum of views.

At one extreme, sociologists have clung to the earlier, simpler solutions to the various epistemological problems, even where these answers are now commonly recognised by philosophers to be inadequate. In other words, they have continued to pursue a programme aimed at constructing a natural science of society centring on causal laws derived from or tested by observational data with the aid of statistical techniques, and they treat the philosophical problems as mere technical difficulties in the manner touched on at the end of Chapter 3. Among this group of statistical technicians, doubts about positivist presuppositions in social analysis are assumed to be resolvable by greater attention to the details of data collection and statistical techniques.

At the other extreme, sociologists have taken the philosophical problems as grounds for rejecting the concerns of positivist philosophers altogether, and they have turned instead to anti-positivist programmes for sociological analysis and research. Indeed, attempts to establish any sort of positivist hegemony in sociology have always faced numerous challenges that alternative understandings of the social world are more appropriate to the human nature of its subject matter. What is of interest here is not whether any of these challenges are successful or whether positivism of some sort is able to disarm or absorb them, but that the challengers take positivism as their target, still assuming that it is the dominant form of sociology to be discredited and transcended by their preferred alternative.

Positivism may be dead in that there is no longer an indentifiable community of philosophers who give its simpler characterisations unqualified support, but it lives on philosophically, developed until it transmutes into conventionalism or realism. And even if in its simpler philosophical forms it is dead, the spirit of those earlier formulations continues to haunt sociology, in a full range of guises, from the sociological technicians' programme for a natural science of society, pursued through increasingly

sophisticated statistical manipulation of carefully quantified data, to the perhaps mythical belief that sociology's
most urgent need is to be liberated from domination by
positivism.

Bibliography

In this bibliography I have included important original works, together with secondary sources where arguments and interpretations I have relied upon are more fully developed. The date given immediately after an author's name is the original date of publication of the title listed. (The original work was sometimes a foreign language edition and sometimes a version that was subsequently revised.) The date of the version I have consulted and from which page references in the text are taken, if different from the date of the original work, is given after the publisher's name.

Abel, T. (1948), 'The operation called *verstehen*', *American Journal of Sociology*, vol. 59, pp. 211–18.

Abell, P. (1971), *Model Building in Sociology* (New York: Schocken).

Abrams, M. (1951), *Social Surveys and Social Action* (London: Heinemann).

Abrams, P. (1968), *The Origins of British Sociology* (Chicago: University of Chicago Press).

Achinstein, P. (1971), *Law and Explanation: An Essay in the Philosophy of Science* (London: OUP).

Anscombe, G. E. M. (1971), *Causality and Determination* (Cambridge: CUP).

Atkins, L., and Jarrett, D. (1979), 'The significance of "significance tests"', in *Demystifying Social Statistics*, ed. J. Irvine, I. Miles and J. Evans (London: Pluto Press), pp. 87–109.

Austin, J. L. (1962), *Sense and Sensibilia* (Oxford: Clarendon Press).

Ayer, A. J. (1936), *Language, Truth and Logic* (Harmondsworth: Penguin, 1971).

Ayer, A. J. (1946), 'Introduction' to his *Language, Truth and Logic*, 2nd edn (Harmondsworth: Penguin, 1971), pp. 7–35.

Ayer, A. J. (1959), 'Editor's introduction' to his *Logical Positivism* (Glencoe, Ill.: The Free Press).

Ayer, A. J. (1967), 'Man as a subject for science', in *Philosophy, Politics and Society*, 3rd ser., ed. P. Laslett and W. R. Runciman (Oxford: Blackwell), pp. 6–24.

Becker, C. L. (1932), *The Heavenly City of the Eighteenth-Century Philosophers* (New Haven, Conn.: Yale University Press).

Becker, H., and Barnes, H. E. (1938), *Social Thought: From Lore to Science* (New York: Dover, 1961).

Benoit-Smullyan, E. (1948), 'The sociologism of Emile Durkheim and his school', in *An Introduction to the History of Sociology*, ed. H. E. Barnes (Chicago: University of Chicago Press, 1950), pp. 499–537.

Benton, T. (1977), *Philosophical Foundations of the Three Sociologies* (London: Routledge & Kegan Paul).

Berelson, B., and Steiner, G. A. (1964), *Human Behaviour: An Inventory of Scientific Findings* (New York: Harcourt, Brace & World).

Bhaskar, R. (1975), *A Realist Theory of Science*, 2nd edn (Hassocks: Harvester Press, 1978).

Bhaskar, R. (1979), *The Possibility of Naturalism: A Philosophical Critique of the Contemporary Human Sciences* (Brighton: Harvester Press).

Black, J. A., and Champion, D. J. (1976), *Methods and Issues in Social Research* (New York: Wiley).

Black, M. (1954), '"Pragmatic" justification of induction', in his *Problems of Analysis: Philosophical Essays* (London: Routledge & Kegan Paul), pp. 157–90.

Blalock, H. M. (1960), *Social Statistics* (New York: McGraw-Hill).

Blalock, H. M. (1964), *Causal Inferences in Nonexperimental Research* (Chapel Hill, NC: University of North Carolina Press).

Blalock, H. M. (1969), *Theory Construction: From Verbal to Mathematical Formulations* (Englewood Cliffs, NJ: Prentice-Hall).

Blumberg, A. E. and Feigl, H. (1931), 'Logical positivism: a new movement in European philosophy', *Journal of Philosophy*, vol. 28, pp. 281–96.

Booth, C. (1902–3), *Life and Labour of the People of London*, 17 vols (London: Macmillan).

Bottomore, T. (1979), 'Marxism and sociology', in *A History of Sociological Analysis*, ed. T. Bottomore and R. A. Nisbet (London: Heinemann), pp. 118–48.

Boudon, R. (1968), 'A new look at correlation analysis', in *Methodology in Social Research*, ed. H. M. Blalock and A. B. Blalock (New York: McGraw-Hill), pp. 199–235.

Boudon, R. (1971), *The Logic of Sociological Explanation* (Harmondsworth: Penguin, 1974).

Bowley, A. L. (1913), 'Working-class households in Reading', *Journal of the Royal Statistical Society*, vol. 76, pp. 672–701.

Bowley, A. L., and Burnett-Hurst, A. R. (1915), *Livelihood and Poverty* (London: Bell).

Braithwaite, R. B. (1953), *Scientific Explanation: A Study of the Function of Theory, Probability and Law in Science* (Cambridge: CUP, 1968).

Bridgman, P. W. (1927), *The Logic of Modern Physics* (New York: Macmillan).

Buck, P. (1977), 'Seventeenth-century political arithmetic: civil strife and vital statistics', *Isis*, vol. 68, pp. 67–84.

Burks, A. W. (1977), *Cause, Chance and Reason* (Chicago: University of Chicago Press).

Carnap, R. (1928), *The Logical Structure of the World* (London: Routledge & Kegan Paul, 1967).

Carnap, R. (1930), 'The old and the new logic', in *Logical Positivism*, ed. A. J. Ayer (Glencoe, Ill.: The Free Press, 1959), pp. 133–46.

Carnap, R. (1932a), 'The elimination of metaphysics through logical analysis of language', in *Logical Positivism*, ed. A. J. Ayer (Glencoe, Ill.: The Free Press, 1959), pp. 60–81.

Carnap, R. (1932b), 'Psychology in physical language', in *Logical Positivism*, ed. A. J. Ayer (Glencoe, Ill.: The Free Press, 1959), pp. 165–98.

Carnap, R. (1934), *The Unity of Science* (London: Kegan Paul, Trench, Trubner).

Carnap, R. (1936–7), 'Testability and meaning', *Philosophy of Science*, vol. 3, pp. 420–68, vol. 4, pp. 1–40.

Carnap, R. (1945), 'The two concepts of probability', *Philosophy and Phenomenological Research*, vol. 5, pp. 513–32.

Carnap, R. (1950), *Logical Foundations of Probability* (Chicago: University of Chicago Press).

Carnap, R. (1966), *Philosophical Foundations of Physics* (New York: Basic Books).

Clark, T. N. (1973), *Prophets and Patrons: The French University and the Emergence of the Social Sciences* (Cambridge, Mass.: Harvard University Press).

Cole, J. R. (1979), *Fair Science: Women in the Scientific Community* (New York: The Free Press).

Cole, S. (1972), 'Continuity and institutionalisation in science: a case study of failure', in *The Establishment of Empirical Sociology: Studies in Continuity, Discontinuity and Institutionalisation*, ed. A. Oberschall (New York: Harper & Row), pp. 73–129.

Collini, S. (1979), *Liberalism and Sociology* (Cambridge: CUP).

Comte, A. (1822), 'Plan of the scientific operations necessary for reorganising society', in his *Early Essays on Social Philosophy* (London: George Routledge, n.d.), pp. 88–217.

Comte, A. (1824), 'Philosophical considerations on the sciences and men of science', in his *Early Essays in Social Philosophy* (London: George Routledge, n.d.), pp. 218–75.

Comte, A. (1830), *Introduction to Positive Philosophy* (Indianapolis, Ind.: Bobbs-Merrill, 1970).

Comte, A. (1830–42), *Cours de philosophie positive*, 6 vols (Paris: Bachelier).

Comte, A. (1851–4), *Système de politique positive ou traité de sociologie* (Paris: Mathias).

Comte, A. (1877), *Cours de philosophie positive*, Vol. 4, 4th edn (Paris: Ballière).

Davidson, D. (1963), 'Actions, reasons and causes', *Journal of Philosophy*, vol. 60, pp. 685–700.

Davidson, D. (1980), *Essays on Actions and Events* (Oxford: Clarendon Press).

DES (1978), *Higher Education in the 1990s: A Discussion Document* (London: DES, February).

Donagan, A. (1964), 'Historical explanation: the Popper–Hempel theory reconsidered', *History and Theory*, vol. 4, pp. 3–26.

Dudycha, A. L., and Dudycha, L. W. (1972), 'Behavioural statistics: an historical perspective', in *Statistical Issues: A Reader for the Behavioural Sciences*, ed. R. E. Kirk (Monterey, Calif.: Brooks/Cole), pp. 2–25.

Duhem, P. (1906), *The Aim and Structure of Physical Theory* (Princeton, NJ: Princeton University Press, 1954).

Duncan, O. D. (1966), 'Path analysis: sociological examples', *American Journal of Sociology*, vol. 72, pp. 1–16.

Durkheim, E. (1897), *Suicide: A Study in Sociology* (London: Routledge & Kegan Paul, 1952).

Durkheim, E., and Fauconnet, P. (1903), 'Sociologie et sciences sociales', *Revue philosophique*, vol. 55, pp. 465–97.

Feigl, H. (1952), 'Validation and vindication', in *Readings in Ethical Theory*, ed. W. Sellars and J. Hospers (New York: Appleton-Century-Crofts), pp. 667–80.

Feigl, H. (1969a), 'The origin and spirit of logical positivism', in *The Legacy of Logical Positivism: Studies in the Philosophy of Science*, ed. P. Achinstein and S. F. Barker (Baltimore, Md: Johns Hopkins University Press), pp. 3–24.

Feigl, H. (1969b), 'The Wiener Kreis in America', in *The Intellectual Migration: Europe and America, 1930–1960*, ed. D. Fleming and B. Bailyn (Cambridge, Mass.: Harvard University Press), pp. 630–73.

Feigl, H. (1970), 'The "orthodox" view of theories: remarks in defense as well as critique', in *Minnesota Studies in the Philosophy of Science*, Vol. 4, ed. M. Radner and S. Winokur (Minneapolis, Minn.: University of Minnesota Press), pp. 3–16.

Fisher, R. A. (1925), *Statistical Methods for Research Workers*, 6th edn (Edinburgh: Oliver & Boyd, 1936).

Fisher, R. A. (1930), 'Inverse probability', *Proceedings of the Cambridge Philosophical Society*, vol. 26, pp. 528–35.

Galton, F. (1865), 'Hereditary talent and character', *Macmillan's Magazine*, vol. 12, pp. 157–66, 318–27.

Galton, F. (1889), *Natural Inheritance* (London: Macmillan).

Galtung, J. (1967), *Theory and Methods of Social Research* (Oslo: Universitetsförlaget).

Glazer, N. (1959), 'The rise of social research in Europe', in *The*

Human Meaning of the Social Sciences, ed. D. Lerner (New York: Meridian Books), pp. 43–72.

Glymour, C. (1980), *Theory and Evidence* (Princeton, NJ: Princeton University Press).

Goodman, N. (1963), 'The significance of *Der Logische Aufbau der Welt*', in *The Philosophy of Rudolf Carnap*, ed. P. A. Schlipp (La Salle, Ill.: Open Court), pp. 545–58.

Graunt, J. (1662), *Natural and Political Observations made upon the Bills of Mortality by John Graunt* (Gregg International, 1973).

Hacking, I. (1975), *The Emergence of Probability: A Philosophical Study of Early Ideas about Probability, Induction and Statistical Inference* (Cambridge: CUP).

Hanfling, O. (1981), *Logical Positivism* (Oxford: Blackwell).

Harré, R. (1961), *Theories and Things: A Brief Study in Prescriptive Metaphysics* (London: Sheed & Ward).

Harré, R. (1970), *The Principles of Scientific Thinking* (London: Macmillan).

Harré, R., and Madden, E. H. (1975), *Causal Powers: A Theory of Natural Necessity* (Oxford: Blackwell).

Harré, R., and Secord, P. F. (1972), *The Explanation of Social Behaviour* (Oxford: Blackwell).

Hawthorne, G. (1976), *Enlightenment and Despair: A History of Sociology* (Cambridge: CUP).

Hazard, P. (1954), *European Thought in the Eighteenth Century* (New Haven, Conn.: Yale University Press).

Hempel, C. G. (1935), 'The logical analysis of psychology', in *Readings in Philosophical Analysis*, ed. H. Feigl and W. Sellars (New York: Appleton-Century-Crofts, 1949), pp. 373–84.

Hempel, C. G. (1942), 'The function of general laws in history', *Journal of Philosophy*, vol. 39, pp. 35–48.

Hempel, C. G. (1958), 'The theoretician's dilemma', in *Minnesota Studies in the Philosophy of Science*, Vol. 2, ed. H. Feigl, M. Scriven and G. Maxwell (Minneapolis, Minn.: University of Minnesota Press), pp. 37–98.

Hempel, C. G. (1965a), 'Aspects of scientific explanation', in his *Aspects of Scientific Explanation* (New York: The Free Press), pp. 331–496.

Hempel, C. G. (1965b), 'Empiricist criteria of cognitive significance: problems and changes', in his *Aspects of Scientific Explanation* (New York: The Free Press), pp. 101–19.

Hempel, C. G. (1969), 'Logical positivism and the social sciences', in *The Legacy of Logical Positivism: Studies in the Philosophy of Science*, ed. P. Achinstein and S. F. Barker (Baltimore, Md: Johns Hopkins University Press), pp. 163–94.

Hempel, C. G. (1970) 'On the "standard conception" of scientific theories', in *Minnesota Studies in the Philosophy of Science*, Vol. 4, ed. M. Radner and S. Winokur (Minneapolis, Minn.: University of Minnesota Press), pp. 142–63.

Hempel, C. G., and Oppenheim, P. (1948), 'Studies in the logic of explanation', *Philosophy of Science*, vol. 15, pp. 135–75.

Hilts, V. L. (1973), 'Statistics and social science', in *Foundations of Scientific Method: The Nineteenth Century*, ed. R. N. Giere and R. S. Westfall (Bloomington, Ind.: Indiana University Press), pp. 206–33.

Hintikka, J. (1968), 'Induction by enumeration and induction by elimination', in *The Problem of Inductive Logic*, ed. I. Lakatos (Amsterdam: North-Holland), pp. 191–216.

Hofstadter, R. (1955), *Social Darwinism in American Thought, 1860–1915* (Boston, Mass.: Beacon Press).

Homans, G. C. (1961), *Social Behaviour: Its Elementary Forms*, 2nd edn (New York: Harcourt, Brace & World, 1974).

Homans, G. C. (1964), 'Contemporary theory in sociology', in *Handbook of Modern Sociology*, ed. R. E. L. Faris (Chicago: Rand McNally), pp. 951–77.

Homans, G. C. (1967), *The Nature of Social Science* (New York: Harcourt, Brace & World).

Hughes, H. S. (1958), *Consciousness and Society: The Reorientation of European Social Thought, 1890–1930* (London: MacGibbon & Kee, 1967).

Joergensen, J. (1951), 'The development of logical positivism', *International Encyclopedia of Unified science. Vol. 2, No. 1: Foundations of the Social Sciences* (Chicago: University of Chicago Press).

Johansson, I. (1975), *A Critique of Karl Popper's Methodology* (Stockholm: Akademiförlaget).

Joynt, C. B., and Rescher, N. (1959), 'On explanation in history', *Mind*, vol. 68, pp. 383–8.

Kaplan, A. (1964), *The Conduct of Inquiry* (Scranton, Penn.: Chandler).

Keat, R., and Urry, J. (1975), *Social Theory as Science* (London: Routledge & Kegan Paul).

Kenny, A. J. P. (1963), *Action, Emotion and Will* (London: Routledge & Kegan Paul).

Kenny, D. A. (1979), *Correlation and Causality* (New York: Wiley).

Keynes, J. M. (1921), *A Treatise on Probability* (London: Macmillan).

Kim, J. (1971), 'Causes and events: Mackie on causation', *Journal of Philosophy*, vol. 68, pp. 426–41.

Kneale, W. (1950), 'Natural laws and contrary-to-fact conditionals', *Analysis*, vol. 10, pp. 121–5.

Kolakowski, L. (1966), *Positivist Philosophy: From Hume to the Vienna Circle* (Harmondsworth: Penguin, 1972).

Kraft, V. (1953), *The Vienna Circle: The Origin of Neo-Positivism* (New York: Philosophical Library).

Kyburg, H. E. (1974), 'Propensity and probabilities', *British Journal for the Philosophy of Science*, vol. 24, pp. 358–75.

Lakatos, I. (1970), 'Falsification and the methodology of scientific research programmes', in *Criticism and the Growth of Knowledge*, ed. I. Lakatos and A. Musgrave (Cambridge: CUP), pp. 91–196.

Lazarsfeld, P. F. (1948), 'The use of panels in social research', *Proceedings of the American Philosophical Society*, vol. 92, pp. 405–10.

Lazarsfeld, P. F. (1955), 'The interpretation of statistical relations as a research operation', in *The Language of Social Research*, ed. P. F. Lazarsfeld and M. Rosenberg (New York: The Free Press), pp. 115–25.

Lazarsfeld, P. F. (1961), 'Notes on the history of quantification in sociology – trends, sources and problems', *Isis*, vol. 52, pp. 277–333.

Lazarsfeld, P. F. (1969), 'An episode in the history of social research: a memoir', in *The Intellectual Migration: Europe and America, 1930–1960*, ed. D. Fleming and B. Bailyn (Cambridge, Mass.: Harvard University Press), pp. 270–337.

Lazarsfeld, P. F., and Oberschall, A. (1965), 'Max Weber and empirical social research', *American Sociological Review*, vol. 30, pp. 185–99.

Lazerwitz, B. (1968), 'Sampling theory and procedures', in *Methodology in Social Research*, ed. H. B. Blalock and A. B. Blalock (New York: McGraw-Hill), pp. 278–328.

Lessnoff, M. H. (1974), *The Structure of Social Science: A Philosophical Introduction* (London: Allen & Unwin).

Levison, A. B. (1974), *Knowledge and Society: An Introduction to the Philosophy of the Social Sciences* (Indianapolis, Ind.: Bobbs-Merrill).

Lofland, J. (1971), *Analysing Social Settings: A Guide to Qualitative Observation and Analysis* (Belmont, Calif.: Wadsworth).

Losee, J. (1972), *A Historical Introduction to the Philosophy of Science* (London: OUP).

Louch, A. R. (1966), *Explanation and Human Action* (Oxford: Blackwell).

Lukes, S. (1973), *Emile Durkheim: His Life and Work: A Historical and Critical Study* (Harmondsworth: Penguin).

Mach, E. (1883), *The Science of Mechanics* (Chicago: Open Court, 1902).

Mach, E. (1886), *The Analysis of Sensations and the Relation of the Physical to the Psychical* (Chicago: Open Court, 1914).

MacKenzie, D. (1979), 'Eugenics and the rise of mathematical statistics in Britain', in *Demystifying Social Statistics*, ed. J. Irvine, I. Miles and J. Evans (London: Pluto Press), pp. 39–50.

MacKenzie, D., and Barnes, B. (1979), 'Scientific judgement: the biometry–Mendelism controversy', in *Natural Order*, ed. B. Barnes and S. Shapin (London: Sage), pp. 191–210.

Mackie, J. L. (1965), 'Causes and conditions', *American Philosophical Quarterly*, vol. 2, pp. 245–64.

Mackie, J. L. (1974), *The Cement of the Universe: A Study of Causation* (London: OUP).

McMullin, E. (1970), 'The history and philosophy of science: a taxonomy', in *Minnesota Studies in the Philosophy of Science*, Vol. 5, ed. R. H. Stuewer (Minneapolis, Minn.: University of Minnesota Press), pp. 12–67.

Marcuse, H. (1941), *Reason and Revolution* (London: Routledge & Kegan Paul, 1969).

Martindale, D. (1961), *The Nature and Types of Sociological Theory* (London: Routledge & Kegan Paul).

Meldon, A. I. (1961), *Free Action* (London: Routledge & Kegan Paul).

Mill, J. S. (1843), *A System of Logic* (London: Longman, 1961).

Moore, G. E. (1903), *Principia Ethica* (Cambridge: CUP).

Morris, C. (1937), *Logical Positivism, Pragmatism and Scientific Empiricism* (Paris: Herman & Cie).

Morrison, D. E., and Henkel, R. E. (1970), *The Significance Test Controversy: A Reader* (London: Butterworth).

Mullins, N. C. (1973), *Theory and Theory Groups in Contemporary American Sociology* (New York: Harper & Row).

Nagel, E. (1961), *The Structure of Science: Problems in the Logic of Scientific Explanation* (London: Routledge & Kegan Paul).

Neurath, O. (1931a), 'Sociology and physicalism', in *Logical Positivism*, ed. A. J. Ayer (Glencoe, Ill.: The Free Press, 1959), pp. 282–317.

Neurath, O. (1931b), 'Empirical sociology: the scientific content of history and political economy', in *Empiricism and Sociology*, ed. M. Neurath and R. S. Cohen (Dordrecht: Reidel, 1973), pp. 319–421.

Neurath, O. (1944), 'Foundations of the social sciences', *International Encyclopedia of Unified Science. Vol. 2, No. 1: Foundations of the Social Sciences* (Chicago: University of Chicago Press).

Neurath, O., Hahn, H., and Carnap, R. (1929), 'The scientific conception of the world: the Vienna Circle', in *Empiricism and Sociology*, ed. M. Neurath and R. S. Cohen (Dordrecht: Reidel, 1973), pp. 299–318.

Neyman, J. (1934), 'On the two different aspects of the representative method: the method of stratified sampling and the method of purposive selection', *Journal of the Royal Statistical Society*, vol. 109, pp. 558–606.

Neyman, J. (1937), 'Outline of a theory of statistical estimation based on the classical theory of probability', *Royal Society of London Philosophical Transactions*, vol. 236, pp. 333–80.

Nisbet, R. A. (1967), *The Sociological Tradition* (London: Heinemann).

Nisbet, R. A. (1973), *The Social Philosophers* (New York: Thomas Y. Crowell).

Oberschall, A. (1965), *Empiricist Social Research in Germany, 1848–1914* (Paris: Mouton).

Oberschall, A. (1972a), 'Introduction: the sociological study of the history of social research', in *The Establishment of Empirical*

Sociology: Studies in Continuity, Discontinuity and Institutionalisation, ed. A. Oberschall (New York: Harper & Row), pp. 1–14.

Oberschall, A. (1972b), 'The institutionalisation of American sociology', in *The Establishment of Empirical Sociology: Studies in Continuity, Discontinuity and Institutionalisation*, ed. A. Oberschall (New York: Harper & Row), pp. 187–251.

Outhwaite, W. (1975), *Understanding Social Life: The Method Called Verstehen* (London: Allen & Unwin).

Parsons, T. (1937), *The Structure of Social Action: A Study in Social Theory with Special Reference to a Group of Recent European Writers* (New York: The Free Press).

Passmore, J. (1957), *A Hundred Years of Philosophy* (Harmondsworth: Penguin, 1968).

Pearson, E. S. (1938), *Karl Pearson: An Appreciation of Some Aspects of his Life and Work* (Cambridge: CUP).

Peel, J. D. Y. (1971), *Herbert Spencer: The Evolution of a Sociologist* (London: Heinemann).

Peirce, C. S. (1878), 'How to make our ideas clear', *Popular Science Monthly*, vol. 12, pp. 286–302.

Peirce, C. S. (1883), 'A theory of probable inference', in *Collected Papers of Charles Sanders Peirce*, Vol. 2, ed. C. Hartshorne, P. Weiss and A. Burks (Cambridge, Mass.: Harvard University Press), pp. 433–77.

Peters, R. S. (1958), *The Concept of Motivation* (London: Routledge & Kegan Paul).

Phillips, D. L. (1973), *Abandoning Method: Sociological Studies in Methodology* (San Francisco: Jossey-Bass).

Popper, K. R. (1934), *The Logic of Scientific Discovery* (London: Hutchinson, 1975).

Popper, K. R. (1944–5), *The Poverty of Historicism*, 2nd edn (London: Routledge & Kegan Paul, 1961).

Popper, K. R. (1963), *Conjectures and Refutations: The Growth of Scientific Knowledge*, 3rd edn (London: Routledge & Kegan Paul, 1969).

Popper, K. (1978), *Unended Quest* (London: Fontana).

Putnam, H. (1962), 'What theories are not', in *Logic, Methodology and Philosophy of Science: Proceedings of the 1960 International Congress*, ed. E. Nagel, P. Suppes and A. Tarski (Stanford, Calif.: Stanford University Press), pp. 240–51.

Quételet, A. (1835), *Sur l'homme et le développement de ses facultés, ou essai de physique sociale* (Paris: Bachelier).

Radnitzky, G. (1968), *Contemporary Schools of Metascience: Vol. 1, Anglo-Saxon Schools of Metascience* (Göteborg: Akademiförlaget).

Reichenbach, H. (1936), 'Logistic empiricism in Germany and the present state of its problems', *Journal of Philosophy*, no. 6, pp. 141–60.

Reichenbach, H. (1938), *Experience and Prediction* (Chicago: University of Chicago Press).

Reichenbach, H. (1949), 'The justification of induction', in his *The Theory of Probability* (Berkeley, Calif.: University of California Press), pp. 469–82.

Reichenbach, H. (1954), *Nomological Statements and Admissible Operations* (Amsterdam: North-Holland).

Rowntree, B. S. (1941), *Poverty and Progress: A Second Social Survey of York* (London: Longmans, Green).

Rowntree, B. S., and Lavers, G. R. (1951), *Poverty and the Welfare State: A Third Social Survey of York, dealing only with Economic Questions* (London: Longmans, Green).

Rudner, R. S. (1966), *Philosophy of Social Science* (Englewood Cliffs, NJ: Prentice-Hall).

Runciman, W. G. (1965), *Social Science and Political Theory* (Cambridge: CUP).

Russell, B. (1917), *Mysticism and Logic*, 2nd edn (London: Allen & Unwin, 1929).

Ryle, G. (1949), *The Concept of Mind* (Harmondsworth: Penguin, 1963).

Salmon, W. (1961), 'Vindication and induction', in *Current Issues in the Philosophy of Science*, ed. H. Feigl and G. E. Maxwell (New York: Holt, Rinehart & Winston), pp. 245–56.

Schlick, M. (1918), *General Theory of Knowledge* (Vienna: Springer-Verlag, 1974).

Scriven, M. (1966), 'Causes, connections, and conditions in history', in *Philosophical Analysis and History*, ed. W. H. Dray (New York: Harper & Row), pp. 238–64.

Searle, J. R. (1972), *Speech Acts* (Cambridge: CUP).

Selvin, H. C. (1976), 'Durkheim, Booth and Yule: the non-diffusion of an intellectual innovation', *European Journal of Sociology*, vol. 17, pp. 39–51.

Seng, Y. P. (1951), 'Historical survey of the development of sampling theories and practice', *Journal of the Royal Statistical Society*, vol. 114, pp. 214–31.

Shaw, M., and Miles, I. (1979), 'The social roots of statistical knowledge', in *Demystifying Social Statistics*, ed. J. Irvine, I. Miles and J. Evans (London: Pluto Press), pp. 27–38.

Siegel, S. (1956), *Non-parametric Statistics for the Behavioural Sciences* (New York: McGraw-Hill).

Simon, H. A. (1954), 'Spurious correlation: a causal interpretation', *Journal of the American Statistical Association*, vol. 49, pp. 467–79.

Simon, W. M. (1963), *European Positivism in the Nineteenth Century* (New York: Cornell University Press).

Smith, H. W. (1975), *Strategies of Social Research: The Methodological Imagination* (Englewood Cliffs, NJ: Prentice-Hall).

Spencer, H. (1857), 'Progress: its law and cause', in *Herbert Spencer on Social Evolution: Selected Writings*, ed. J. D. Y. Peel (Chicago: University of Chicago Press, 1972), pp. 38–52.

Spencer, H. (1864), 'Reasons for dissenting from the philosophy of M. Comte', appended to his *The Classification of the Sciences* (London: Williams & Norgate), pp. 27–48.

Stephan, F. S. (1948), 'History of the uses of modern sampling procedures', *Journal of the American Statistical Association*, vol. 43, pp. 12–39.

Sterling, T. D. (1959), 'Publication decisions and their possible effects on inferences drawn from tests of significance – or vice versa', *Journal of the American Statistical Association*, vol. 54, pp. 30–4.

Stinchcombe, A. L. (1968), *Constructing Social Theories* (New York: Harcourt, Brace & World).

Stouffer, S. A., Suchman, L. C., DeVinney, L. C., Star, S. A., and Williams, R. M. (1949a), *The American Soldier, Vol. I: Adjustment during Army Life* (Princeton, NJ: Princeton University Press).

Stouffer, S. A., Lumsdaine, A. A., Lumsdaine, M. H., Williams, R. M., Smith, M. B., Janis, I. L., Star, S. A., and Cottrell, L. S. (1949b), *The American Soldier, Vol II: Combat and its Aftermath* (Princeton, NJ: Princeton University Press).

Strawson, P. F. (1952), 'The "justification" of induction', in his *Introduction to Logical Theory* (London: Methuen), pp. 248–63.

Studdert-Kennedy, G. (1975), *Evidence and Explanation in Social Science: An Interdisciplinary Approach* (London: Routledge & Kegan Paul).

Suppe, F. (1977), 'Afterword', in *The Structure of Scientific Theories*, 2nd edn, ed. F. Suppe (Urbana, Ill.: University of Illinois Press), pp. 615–730.

Taylor, C. (1964), *The Explanation of Behaviour* (London: Routledge & Kegan Paul).

Taylor, C. C. (1920), 'The social survey and the science of sociology', *American Journal of Sociology*, vol. 25, pp. 731–56.

Taylor, R. (1966), *Action and Purpose* (New York: Humanities Press, 1974).

Timasheff, N. S. (1955), *Sociological Theory: Its Nature and Growth* (New York: Random House).

Tiryakian, E. A. (1979), 'Emile Durkheim', in *A History of Sociological Analysis*, ed. T. Bottomore and R. A. Nisbet (London: Heinemann), pp. 187–236.

Torrance, J. (1976), 'The emergence of sociology in Austria, 1885–1935', *European Journal of Sociology*, vol. 17, pp. 185–219.

Toulmin, S. (1953), *The Philosophy of Science: An Introduction* (London: Hutchinson).

Upshaw, H. S. (1968), 'Attitude measurement', in *Methodology in Social Research*, ed. H. M. Blalock and A. B. Blalock (New York: McGraw-Hill), pp. 60–111.

Von Mises, R. (1928), *Probability, Statistics and Truth* (London: William Hodge, 1939).

Walker, H. M. (1929), *Studies in the History of Statistical Method* (Baltimore, Md: Williams & Wilkins).

Wallace, W. L. (1971), *The Logic of Science in Sociology* (Chicago: Aldine-Atherton).

Weber, M. (1914), *The Theory of Social and Economic Organisation* (New York: The Free Press, 1964).

Westergaard, H. L. (1932), *Contributions to the History of Statistics* (London: P. S. King & Son).

Whitehead, A. N., and Russell, B. (1910–13), *Principia Mathematica*, 3 vols (Cambridge: CUP).

Williams, R. M. (1947), *The Reduction of Intergroup Tensions: A Survey of Research on Problems of Ethnic, Racial, and Religious Group Relations*, Bulletin No. 57 (New York: Social Science Research Council).

Winch, P. (1958), *The Idea of a Social Science and Its Relation to Philosophy* (London: Routledge & Kegan Paul).

Wittgenstein, L. (1921), *Tractatus Logico-Philosophicus* (London: Routledge & Kegan Paul, 1961).

Wittgenstein, L. (1953), *Philosophical Investigations*, 2nd edn (Oxford: Blackwell, 1958).

Worsley, P. M. W. (ed.) (1970), *Introducing Sociology*, 2nd edn (Harmondsworth: Penguin, 1977).

Yule, G. U. (1895), 'On the correlation of total pauperism with proportion of out-relief', *Economic Journal*, vol. 5, pp. 601–11.

Zeller, R. A., and Carmines, E. G. (1980), *Measurement in the Social Sciences: The Link Between Theory and Data* (Cambridge: CUP).

Zetterberg, H. L. (1954), *On Theory and Verification in Sociology*, 3rd edn (Totowa, NJ: Bedminster Press, 1965).

INDEX